THE FABRIC LOVER'S SCRAPBOOK

Other books in the Creative Machine Arts Series,
available from Chilton:

The Complete Book of Machine Embroidery
    by Robbie and Tony Fanning

Creative Nurseries Illustrated
    by Debra Terry and Juli Plooster

Creative Serging Illustrated
    by Pati Palmer, Gail Brown and Sue Green

The Expectant Mother's Wardrobe Planner
    by Rebecca Dumlao.

Friendship Quilts by Hand and Machine
    by Carolyn Vosburg Hall

Know Your Bernina
    by Jackie Dodson

Pizzazz for Pennies
    by Barb Forman

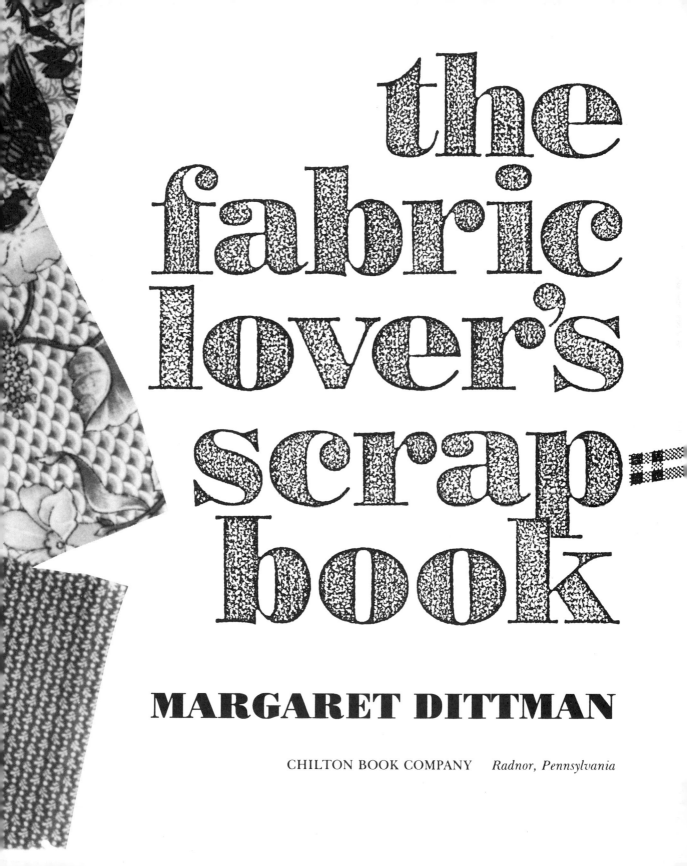

the fabric lover's scrapbook

MARGARET DITTMAN

CHILTON BOOK COMPANY   *Radnor, Pennsylvania*

For my grandmother, Delpha Anne Elizabeth Taylor,
who taught me the art;
and for my mother, Golda Marie Cooper,
who taught me the craft.

Designed by Adrianne Onderdonk Dudden
All black-and-white photographs, except where otherwise noted,
were taken by Scott Lennox and are used here with the kind permission
of PSC Publications.
Manufactured in the United States of America

Library of Congress Cataloging in Publication Data
Dittman, Margaret.
*   The fabric lover's scrapbook.*
*   (Creative machine arts series)*
*   Bibliography: p. 172*
*   Includes index.*
*   1. Textile crafts. I. Title.   II. Series.*
TT699.D58 1987   746   87-47730
ISBN 0-8019-7783-5

3 4 5 6 7 8 9 0   7 6 5 4 3 2 1 0 9 8

CONTENTS

strips

bits

8 QUILTS

9 APPLIQUE

10 CLOTHING

11 HOUSEHOLD ITEMS

trash

scrap happy

FOREWORD

A few years ago a friend of mine was asked to dispose of the household furnishings of a woman who had died suddenly. The deceased, a wealthy woman who lived on the 17-Mile Drive in Pebble Beach, California, loved all forms of needlework, especially sewing and quilting.

When my friend went into the workroom, she found floor-to-ceiling towers of boxes, neatly labelled "Floss," "Pearl Cotton," "Machine-embroidery Thread" and such. But my friend's favorite stack was labelled "Scraps Too Small To Use."

This is an affliction peculiar to those of us who love fabric. We cannot bear to part with the leftovers (most of us also have refrigerators full of tiny jars — a leftover dab of this, a spoonful of that).

I'd like to send that lady's boxes to Margaret Dittman as a challenge: Margaret is a writer who has found a use for every scrap, no matter how small. In fact, in this book she organizes what to do with scraps by how big they are — strips, bits, or trash. She shows you how to use your scraps to make fabric flowers, quilts, fabric jewelry, rugs, and hundreds of other items. She even shows you how to sort and store your hoard.

In her job as co-editor of American HomeArts/Needlecraft for Today (formerly Needle & Thread), Margaret is a magnet for the work of creative designers who use scraps. She shares these clever ideas in a Scrap Bag Gallery.

The good news for you is that you will finish this book inspired to make scrap crafts for yourself and others. The bad news for me is that since working on this book, I have not been able to throw or give away any scraps.

May you always be Scrap Happy!

Robbie Fanning

Series Editor and Co-author,
The Complete Book of Machine Embroidery

Preface

This book was written out of necessity. After a lengthy love affair with fabric and sewing and several major moves during which no fabric was discarded, I discovered that the source of the clutter and disorganization was not the neatly folded three-yard lengths. No, the culprit was those scraps. But I loved them. I'd had some of them since the colorful sixties, when I'd discovered quiltmaking. The question wasn't living without them—it was how to live *with* them.

I'm learning how. It's an ongoing process. Deciding what to keep and how to store it with easy access seems to be a problem with most people who sew, judging from the shrugs, giggles and outright confessions of helplessness from most of my friends and colleagues. There are ideas in Chapter 1 on this challenge.

Scrap sewing is *not* practical. Oh, sure it was for our grandmothers, but just for keeping the baby warm, there's a blanket at the discount store that's far more efficient than anything you'd stitch together with the speediest techniques. No, scrap sewing is frivolous and fun, experimental and exciting. It can easily lead to art. Your baby quilt might turn into a hilarious art piece.

As we talk about techniques for using scraps, art pieces will come up again. Scraps are such a non-threatening way to play with form and color that you'll be led to experiment. Because of this, and because giving specific requirements for a scrap project could quickly grow ridiculous, the projects are generic in nature. My black-and-white might be your multi-color; my miniature, your panorama.

My approach to color is strictly "seat of my pants." This is not, I admit, an elegant term to use in the same breath as color theory. I spent several years in the company of a fine artist who taught me mainly to relax and see what was beautiful. All colors work together, he told me, and gestured broadly at Nature (whatever Nature happened to be at that moment) for affirmation. It was true. If you're out buying yards of fine linen, you'd better be pretty locked-in sure of your color choices and percentages. If you're making a machine-pieced dress yoke, you can watch it develop. If that last green square dulled all the adjacent colors, if it leaps from its neighbors, if it nags at you somehow, you cheerfully rip out your last seam and choose the perfect square. You know what's beautiful. You'll know it when you see it. You probably wouldn't have sewn that last green square on in the first place, would you?

I'm primarily a machine stitcher, and we all know that machine stitching is what produces a vast quantity and variety of scraps in the first place. Yet some of the techniques given here are not sewing machine techniques. Some are for TV-watching, Little League watching, waiting at the airport, and visiting with your grandmother. Unto all things there is a season. There's room in our lives for all kinds of needlework, and there's room in our sewing and storage areas for our precious scraps.

As we touch ever so lightly on these techniques, remember that we're taking a dilettante's approach. This isn't an in-depth study, but an exercise in stretching our minds, our abilities — and that all-important sewing space! You'll probably discover two or three main areas of scrap sewing to be your favorites and find you want to study those realms more deeply. You'll find an assortment of the best books listed in Suggested Reading and a list of suppliers in Sources of Supply.

ACKNOWLEDGMENTS

For supplying materials that aided in researching this book, I'd like to acknowledge and express my thanks to the Viking-Husqvarna Co.; Swiss-Metrosene, Inc.; Thai Silks; Gutcheon Patchworks; Wamsutta Fabrics; Concord Fabrics; Savoir-Faire; Pennywise Fabrics; Stacy

Corp.; Folkwear Patterns; Dritz Corp.; Aardvark Adventures in Handcrafts; and Clearbrook Woolen Shop.

For exquisite modeling, I thank Lacy Dittman, Marra Dittman, Diane Anglim, Melanie Wroten and Holly Jones.

For their consummate skill and good nature, I thank my illustrator, Charlie Davis, and my photographer, John Anglim.

For his cheerful enthusiasm in reading galleys with me, I thank Fred Dittman.

And, of course, dear Robbie, who one day asked innocently, "Do you have a book in you?"

SCRAPS OF WISDOM

If you sew a lot, and if you love fabric, sooner or later you'll wind up in an intricate love-hate relationship with an inescapable byproduct of your sewing—scraps. Scraps can save your life at 11 o'clock some night when you're working feverishly, or they can clutter up your surroundings to the point that you can't find anything. Take this quick test to determine your SQ (scrap quotient):

1. You're making an appliquéd gingham apron for your mother-in-law's birthday, which is tomorrow. Right now, in your sewing room, could you find a small piece of red fabric for an apple appliqué?

2. Could you find a scrap of green for the leaves?

3. When you place your solid white fabric over the gingham to make an apple slice, you discover that you can faintly see the grid of the gingham through the white. Can you find a piece of lightweight muslin or batiste to back the appliqué motif?

4. You're making a simple summer pullover blouse and decide it's entirely too plain. Do you have enough contrasting fabric to bind the sleeve and neckline edges?

5. Your daughter develops an irrational passion for a new jacket to fit her Cabbage Patch doll, Esmerelda. Can you find some woolly or pre-quilted fabric to make the jacket?

6. You have exactly enough fashion fabric to cut your new skirt, but not enough for the side-seam pockets. Can you put your finger on a scrap of fabric suitable for those hidden pockets?

7. It's Thursday morning, and you're at home with a sick child. Your friend telephones with an invitation to a baby shower to be held Friday night. Can you make a gift with materials you have on hand?

8. Do you pause at the remnant bin or counter?

9. Are you known to accept gifts of left-over fabric from friends and relatives?

10. Is your scrap-storage area larger than a bread box?

Give yourself ten points for every "yes" answer to questions 1 through 7. Now subtract ten points for every "yes" answer to questions 8 through 10.

SCORING

70–50   You've worked out a fine system. You'll find some good ideas in this book, but you should really consider writing your own.

40–10   Welcome to the "It's Here Somewhere" Club. You're a fabric lover who needs some help.

Under 10   Don't check this book out of the library; buy a copy for yourself.

HOW THE SORTING SYSTEM WORKS

If you're one of those lucky people who can toss out scraps and never long for them again, you have my congratulations. (Of course you make a lot of trips to the fabric store, too—right?) Most of us serious stitchers do collect left-over scraps, though, and for various reasons. We recognize the elegance in the practice of non-waste; we know we can use that scrap some way, some time. Primarily, though, we love fabric. The best designers and stitchers love fabric. No problem there. The problem arises only when the sheer mass of that fabric becomes such a disorganized mess that you can't find what you're looking for when you need it. I don't care if you own two yards of cinnamon Ultrasuede and three of emerald silk charmeuse; it won't do you any good if you can't put your finger on it. If the disarray in the sewing area becomes overpowering, we have a tendency to avoid that area entirely.

If you make a "scrap" project for every four or five "all-new" projects, you'll be creating attractive and useful items, having a good time, and (almost incidentally) generating a manageable fabric inventory. You won't have to waste time and creative energy clearing surfaces, looking for fabric.

It may seem overwhelming to consider sorting through all your scraps. But you have to do it only once. After you've established your storage system and developed the habit of making scrap projects, it's easy to keep your materials in order. "Order" here means "workable or desirable order." My husband and I have long referred to our style of home furnishing as "creative disarray" or "picturesque clutter." We have no desire for polished, spartan surroundings, and perhaps you agree. But the system should work, and when it doesn't, you don't either. You should be the master of your materials, and not the other way around.

I've been sewing for twenty-five years and have collected fabric for almost that long—everything from old blue jeans to 1-inch squares of silk. From total chaos, I've progressed to reasonable organization, and all without throwing away any of my favorite fabrics. You can, too!

STRIPS, BITS AND TRASH

In a workshop on color for quilters, Mary Ellen Hopkins remarked in an off-hand way that she cuts or tears all her scrap fabric into 1½-inch-wide strips. Though that little gem was almost a throw-away, not at all relevant to the subject at hand, it's what I remember of the day's teaching. In fact, it became the nucleus of my organization plan. "Why," I reasoned later, "limit yourself to strips 1½ inches wide? What if you're left with a strip 2 inches or 3 inches wide? Why narrow it down?" I began "stripping" fabric scraps as wide as the piece of fabric would allow and storing them all together in open, see-through plastic bags. (If fabrics are kept in air-tight containers, moisture can collect and cause damage.) I was making a lot of woven rag rugs at the time and found the pre-cut strips in bags an excellent way to work.

There are hundreds of other uses for strips, from Seminole piecework to fabric fringe, and the strip is often the most efficient way to save scraps. It becomes our first unit in changing clutter to order. Of course, not every scrap of fabric lends itself to stripping.

Strips wouldn't be much use in appliquéing that apple or whipping up Esmerelda's new winter ensemble. And if you found yourself with, say, a 15-inch square of fabric, you'd be narrowing your range of future options if you tore it into 15-inch-long strips. If it's a neat, manageable piece of fabric, leave it as it is. (We'll call these pieces "bits," whether they measure 15 inches or one inch.) The piece at left in Figure 1–1, for instance, should be stripped and the tag ends tossed, while the piece at right is a bit that should be merely trimmed and folded.

One scrap-saver we know folds her smaller bits of fabric into approximate 3-by-5-inch file card-size rectangles and stores them on edge in a box. She can see at a glance what's available.

Nothing is written in stone, however, and if the fabric in either pieces shown were silk, I'd save all the tag ends. Tag ends become bits when you save them.

Our fabric-buying and fabric-saving habits are as individual as ourselves. You might love and use bits of gold lamé that I'd toss; one of our friends may work with tiny prints almost to the exclusion of everything else. I'll confess here and now that I'm a silk freak. I've raised the worms, spun and reeled the cocoons, dyed silk, woven silk, and most of all loved and collected the precious stuff. I'll find a way to use every bit. You may have a passion for fine English woolens, and a tiny piece to you will be worth saving. So we're working here with general guidelines.

To simplify your decision-making process, set a standard like, "I

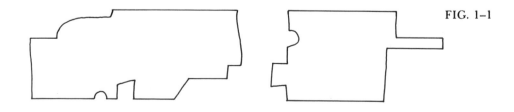

FIG. 1–1

will keep scraps of cotton calico only if they are at least 4 inches square" or "I will not save anything purple. I hate purple." This will save time and mental energy.

As we go through our imaginary typical sewing-room accumulation, we're going to find, in addition to the strips and bits candidates we've already talked about, trash. Trash is fabric you should never have collected in the first place. Although we're not going to throw away anything we like, we'll find a great sense of freedom and momentum in throwing away real trash. But don't be too hasty; there are good uses for the right trash fabrics. A sturdy woven cotton or cotton-blend fabric in even the nastiest of colors can be used in certain ways. Toss the unloved slinky jerseys, the cheap acetates, the coarsely woven fabrics that fray easily—whatever you consider trash—into a box or sack and label it Goodwill, or the name of your favorite local self-help charity. Don't dump it into the collection box yet, though. Finish the book and complete your sorting. You may be in for a big surprise!

HOW TO SORT, PART ONE

The basic rules of sorting can be used in any room of your house. You may become so enamored with total control of your sewing room that you'll decide to extend that euphoric sensation to all your surroundings. We are indebted to Alice Fulton and Pauline Hatch, authors of *It's Here. . .Somewhere!* (see Suggested Reading) for some of the key concepts. Start anywhere, with any shelf or container. Pick up and consider everything. Label four sacks or boxes with the following: "keepers," "junk," "Goodwill," and "somewhere else."

FIG. 1–2

Into the container marked "keepers," of course, you'll place every-thing you want to keep. When you come across larger pieces of fabrics ($^1_2$ yard or more) that don't require edge trimming, just fold them and set them aside. Into "junk," toss genuine throw-aways—tiny scraps, stuff you're sure you don't want to keep. Into the "Goodwill" sack, put things your conscience won't let you throw away. "Somewhere else" will hold pattern pieces, paper clips, the warranty to your refrigerator.

Work around the room clockwise with your containers. When you fill one up, set it aside and label a new container. Remember your guidelines and take a break when you feel your mental gears grating. Work as speedily as you can, remembering that you're going to keep your throw-aways around for a few days or weeks of pondering and possible retrieval.

When you've sorted through everything, throw away your certified junk, set aside or put away the things in your "somewhere else" sack, and hide "Goodwill" from view for a while. Let's deal with "keepers" when we're fresh and adventurous.

HOW TO SORT, PART TWO (GETTING SERIOUS)

Set up your steam iron, padded ironing surface, rotary cutter and mat, scissors, rulers (clear plastic is ideal), and templates. Templates? Sure— and not just for you quilters, either, although *you'll* feel you're in heav-en with a big supply of pre-cut 4-inch squares on hand. Any stitcher will find several sizes of squares and triangles to be a real blessing. I've found that these are my favorite shapes to use in quilts, along with rect-angles, and my best investment lately has been thin brass templates in two sizes of squares and two of triangles. When you come across a bit of fabric that lends itself to the shape, you might as well go ahead and cut some 3-inch squares (or whatever). They'll prove helpful in clothing embellishment, patchwork bands, appliqué bases, and other uses.

You'll also need some containers for your sorted and pressed strips, squares and the like. This is entirely up to you, for you might have an entire room for storage or a small corner. You may be blessed with shelves or make do with a large piece of pegboard and hooks.

Use see-through containers whenever possible. This recommendation is unanimous among my scrap-saving friends. For stacking on shelves, you can't beat clear plastic shoe or sweater boxes from the dimestore. You can see at a glance that this particular box contains, yellow, say, or satin. Of course if you have a huge collection of old blue jeans, you needn't store them in clear containers. A cardboard box with "denim" written on it served me well until I found an old suitcase plastered with gaudy travel stickers. Now I have a mouse-proof denim storage container that's also become a major item of studio decor.

Although fiber content is a vital consideration in most sewing and designing, keeping up with the fiber content of scraps is non-productive. Multiply that clear plastic box times three for all-cotton, polyester-cotton blends, and rayon just to keep up with your yellow scraps? I don't think so. You'll probably let this consideration fall by the wayside, trusting to your memory, discrimination and general good sense.

If you opt for pegboard and hooks, you can make decorative bags (using up some scraps in the process), machine appliqué a visual or verbal clue to the contents, and hang them.

MAKE IT BIG

The ideas in this book do work. Our habits of saving and storing, like any other habits, though, may die hard. It never hurts to play a little

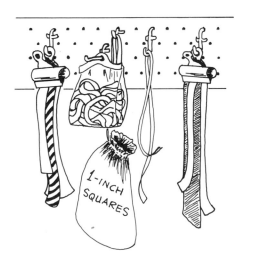

FIG. 1–3

trick on yourself when you know it's for your own good. One little trick to help jar you from your rut is to begin with something that will give you big results, show you a decided difference right away. You could read this book, make a few silk roses (see "Rolled Roses" in Chapter 5), and go right back to your wicked ways. But if you Wallage your wall (see "Wallage" in Chapter 11), or make a shaggy rug (see "Shaggy Rug" in Chapter 6), you're going to notice two big differences: a major project that you can't help but see, and some free, empty space for you to work with. This tangible effect helps galvanize you into a new mindset and makes it easier for you to work in new ways.

FINISHING SCHOOL

A good exercise: Determine to finish something with what you have on hand. Make the exercise more challenging by giving yourself a time limit. We've all been tempted to use orange seam binding on the new turquoise skirt we're aching to wear the next morning—right? And we've promised ourselves we'd correct it later and never did. This is a totally different situation. We're not working with Grandma's paisley shawl or $25 a yard linen.

I did this exercise, and the result was the Seminole Tropics jacket shown in the color section. My "given" was the strip of Seminole piece-work that runs down the sleeves. My challenge was to complete the garment without going to the store. In fact, I wanted the jacket planned and cut that night. There are a lot of things in that jacket I wouldn't have consciously planned to do, asymmetries that forced themselves into the work, fabric juxtapositions that startle. And I love it!

IT'S NOT CHEATING, IT'S PRACTICING

There is nothing wrong with copying someone else's piece. In college this is called an exercise. I attended a workshop with a nationally known needle artist who presented a slide show frankly detailing sources of design for some of her recently finished quilts and garments. Right there along with a Joshua tree and an urban skyline were catalog photographs of Italian sweaters! Of course the designer's completed revised version was nowhere near identical. How much can machine appliqué and beads look like knitted chenille yarn anyway? Don't be afraid to copy if it will get you moving. I've always wanted to see Van Gogh's Starry Night as a fiber art piece, all awash in glitter and beads. Copying is especially helpful it it encourages you to try techniques or materials with which you are unfamiliar. I don't necessarily think it's a blessing, but our years of schooling have resulted in a certain need to be shown how. Set yourself an assignment and go for it. My weaving buddy and I used to set up exercises like that. We'd say, "Let's do rugs with turquoise and brown and beige and make them 2 by 3 feet and meet next month and look at them." Sometimes just the least bit of structure, of guidelines, will release energy and creativity you didn't suspect was there. In the absence of a class or co-learners, be your own teacher.

For years I've been fascinated by the heavily encrusted embroideries that incorporate everything into a richly textured and embroidered surface that seems to breathe with life. Though I long to take needle in hand and do a piece like this, it's not my style. I feel inhibited. But I've solved my dilemma. I'll copy a piece you may have seen or seen photographs of—Memory Jars by Terrie Hancock Mangat of Cincinnati, Ohio. Three simple jar shapes, each heavily embellished, seem to glow upon a minimal background (see *Quilt Digest*, 1985).

My fabrics will be different, my sequins, buttons, faux jewels, appliqués, embroidery stitches; it won't be at all the same, in fact. But I will have my assignment, my parameters, my basic shapes to work with. When I'm done, I won't let people think it's totally original; I'll drop the artist's name frequently. But then, when I envision this same sort of surface embellishment in my own imagination, I won't hesitate to take that needle in hand. I'll be a journeyman.

OPENING DOORS

Welcome any source of inspiration, however irrational. When I heard on Monday that a woman I know would be celebrating her birthday on the next Thursday, I was instantly determined to make her a jacket. "But I can't do that," I argued wisely. "One, I don't know her that well; two, I've got this book to write; and three, my jackets take *hours*." The challenge was there: Design a jacket with what I had on hand so the expense would be negligible (after all, I paid for it last year; therefore it's free now) and make it fast. I had it planned and cut in an hour. During the next couple of days, I realized that I didn't want to give *this* person *this* present—a birthday card was far more suitable to our acquaintance—but that I had another creation painlessly underway. Every time I'd look at the elements all waiting to be assembled, I'd smile, and I sent Pat my good wishes, of course.

If learning that someone you know is pregnant evokes the same automatic response that that news does in me (Baby Quilt!), then go for it. Maybe the child will be in kindergarten before she gets the present, maybe not. That's okay. Use the energy. Seize the moment. There'll be plenty of time later to talk yourself out of it. Doris Dittman, my mother-in-law, has nine grandchildren. When she first discovered cathedral window quilting, she announced her intention of making a quilt in this style for each grandchild. When she'd completed a piece about two feet square, she wisely finished it as a wall hanging and presented it to the family with the most children. But she used that energy!

DON'T GIVE UP TOO SOON

Stretch out. Don't be afraid. Out of fear and ignorance come education and mastery in time. Follow through.

Keep it fun, keep it light. I've tossed several scrap projects into the ragbag, Goodwill sack or trash. Nobody's keeping score. If you're working with $40 a yard silk twill, of course you'll sweat and agonize over it, but if you see that your scrap quilt isn't working, remember to be true to the medium. Before tossing a project out permanently, though, put it aside for a few days or weeks. Often the solution to a problem comes only after we have ceased working actively on it. Remember Elias Howe and his dream of the placement of the eye in the sewing machine needle? After lengthy research and trial and error, he had almost given up in his quest. Up to this point in history, all the needles man had known had eyes near the blunt end. Naturally Mr. Howe had been conditioned by this preconception. Almost at his wit's end, he dreamed one night that he was being pursued by cannibals. As they thrust their spears threateningly in his direction, he saw there were holes in the spears, holes right in the sharp-pointed ends. As soon as he awoke, he raced back to his experiment, relocated the eyes, and the rest is history.

So take a break, give up when necessary, but don't give up too soon. Give the subconscious some credit. Often while you're washing dishes or hoeing the garden, your answer will spring full-blown.

strips

ALL ABOUT STRIPPING

Tools for stripping fabric range from a hand-turned stripper that clamps to a flat surface (about $80) to your fingers (free). The stripper adjusts to different widths, is quite accurate, and can cut through several layers of lightweight fabric with ease. It's a good buy if you develop a preference for one of the scrap crafts which uses a lot of strips; especially rug hooking, which requires very narrow strips, or Seminole piecework, in which accuracy is vital. There are several hand-held tools on the market consisting of adjustable rotary blades set into a handle. Blades can be added and removed. Used with a self-healing mat, these tools are fairly easy to use, but it's necessary to pin the fabric to the mat at intervals, a step I find annoying. There is, of course, the standard one-blade rotary cutter, the most popular models being made by Olfa and Dritz. Once you learn to keep your fingers away from the very serious business end of the rotary cutter, you have a friend for life. Inexpensive, handy, and simple, rotary cutters come in several sizes, even a model with a wave-cut pattern. Use a self-healing mat and a generous-sized ruler with the rotary cutters. I like rulers with those vital parallel lines marked at intervals on clear, strong vinyl. See Fig. 2–1: (A) a stripper that clamps onto a table and cuts through several layers of fabric with ease; (B) stripper for multi-strip cutting; (C) basic rotary cutter. You can cut strips in short order with the rotary cutter, and it's as easy to work with tiny scraps as larger ones. This is not the case with the first two tools we talked about. Self-healing mats come in various sizes, as

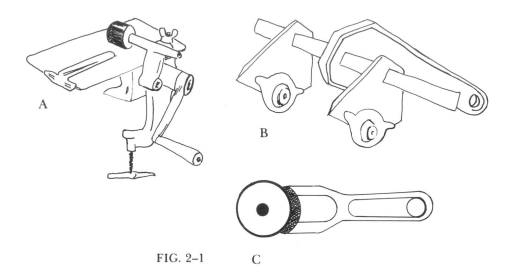

FIG. 2–1   C

well as by the inch or foot. You can now have your entire cutting table covered with this wonder substance.

Less efficient, but certainly feasible if one has to be still a long while anyway, is scissors. Mark lines with a long ruler, then gather up a pile of scraps and watch soap operas while you cut. (Just kidding. But depending on the ages of all your children, you could possibly bribe them to do one or both of these steps for you, or convince them that it's a rare privilege to cut strips; a test of valor and concentration. For many of these techniques, absolute accuracy is not needed.)

If you work in an office or have other access to a paper cutter, you'll find this tool a fast and easy way to cut strips. I haven't practiced enough to become comfortable with it (all right, I'm afraid of it), but I did easily cut eight thicknesses of cotton fabric with one careless swipe. Carol Wien, author of *The Great American Log Cabin Quilt Book* (see Suggested Reading), recommends it highly, advising you cut four layers at a whack.

All these methods can be used to make bias strips, as well as straight-grain strips. Bias binding is a marvelous luxury to have on hand in many colors and widths. As you sort through your scraps, keep possible bias-strip candidates in mind.

For straight-grain strips from relatively large chunks of fabric, snip little cuts in the selvage at intervals and tear. Tearing works best on most light to medium-weight woven fabrics with a high cotton content and for many techniques, though there are some cases when you absolutely demand a hard, cut edge. One major advantage of tearing strips is a guaranteed straight line. Get your children to tear the fabric after you've clipped it. Have them take it outside so you won't have to listen. (There is a story of a Chinese emperor who suffered from oppressive insomnia. He discovered that only the sound of tearing silk could lull him to rest. Night after night slaves ripped precious silks apart in his bedchamber as he drowsed and dreamed.)

STORING STRIPS

After you've pressed and cut your strips, what do you do with them? Depending on the lengths, eventual use and bulk, here are a few ideas:

If heavy cardboard tubes (like the centers from rolls of wide ribbon or tape) are readily available, they're excellent for winding strips onto, but I don't think the effort of finding them or cutting longer cardboard tubes into the right lengths is worthwhile.

You can start winding a strip around two or three fingers as if your fingers were a tube and make a good roll. Secure with a large, stainless-steel pin.

The prettiest way to store strips is just to roll them into a ball like yarn. This, however, is a good method only if it isn't important that the strip remain flat and pressed. It wouldn't do for piecing Seminole strips at all, but it's ideal for weaving rag mats, making rugs on a hairpin-lace loom, etc. In fact, these balls of fabric strips are so very attractive that

FIG. 2–2

fancy shops feature piles of them in baskets as chic home decor accessories.

To keep odd short lengths of strips handy, secure them with a big office clip and hang them where sunshine won't fade the fabric dyes. Or, if slight wrinkling isn't important, wind longer strips around your hand and elbow (just as you'd wind a skein of yarn or an extension cord) and hang on pegboard or other hooks out of direct sunlight.

If practicality is more vital than picturesque charm, just toss rolls, balls and short lengths into clear plastic bags.

SHOULD YOU BE A JOINER?

Some of the strip techniques we'll talk about require continuous lengths, and there are several ways to join strips to produce these. For your initial sorting and storing adventure, though, don't bother. Wait and see what use you'll be making of the strips. Many methods differ, and you may find a craft you like that doesn't demand joining at all.

The easiest, most primitive, and often the most charming method of joining strips is to knot the ends together. This works for rag knitting and crocheting, weaving and certain other techniques.

Sometimes just a line of straight machine stitching over lapped ends of strips will suffice to make a neat appearance and a strong join.

The neatest and strongest method is cutting the ends on the bias (diagonal) or at right angles and machine stitching right sides together. Press seams or not, depending on your project. You can also just overlap the cut ends and run a line of machine stitching through both layers to secure.

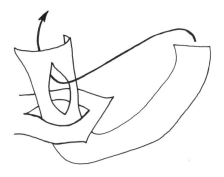

FIG. 2–3

A quick and easy method that produces results almost identical to knotting ends could be called slit-and-slip. Cut ends of strips at a right angle. Cut buttonhole-like slits in both ends of all strips, parallel to the short ends. Slip the end of strip 1 through the slit in strip 2, pull almost all the way through, then slip the farthest end of strip 2 through the slit in its nearest end. This is all shown in Figure 2–3.

Keep the medium in mind—it's scraps, remember—and don't overwork. If tying strips together works as well as cutting and careful seaming, go for the easy, quick way.

Sonya Lee Barrington, well-known as a quilt artist, creates an intricately pieced vest. Photograph by Sharon Risedorph.

Betsy Hatch's appliquéd "Landscape" vest is an excellent example of pieced clothing. Photograph by Betsy Hatch.

Barbara State uses wools and cashmeres for an elegant jumper bib. Photograph by Barbara State.

Folkwear Patterns' Seminole Jacket is pieced with multi-colored silks. Photograph courtesy of Folkwear Patterns.

"Seminole Tropics" combines fabrics and techniques with wild abandon. Designed and sewn by the author. Photograph by John Anglim.

Pieced jacket, "Blues for Charlie," by the author combines Ultrasuede, fringed denim, velvet and calico. Photograph by John Anglim.

Kim Masopust adds traditional quilt blocks to a hand-knit sweater. Photograph by Richard Billings.

Lois Ericson uses woven strips to accent a subtle silk vest. Photograph by John Anglim.

Collaged clothing in its most subtle form: pieced silk tunic by the author; strip-pieced jacket with calla lilies by Vickie Senape; silk T-dress with lattice by Marinda Brown-Stewart. Photograph by John Anglim.

Marinda Brown-Stewart's lavish necklace combines beads, fabric tubes and a medallion. Photograph courtesy of Fairfield Processing Corp.

Fringed sleeves on a kimono-style jacket make a frivolous, light-hearted fashion statement. By the author. Photograph by John Anglim.

Marinda Brown-Stewart interprets her own T-dress pattern with intricate piecing that produces a rich, whole-cloth look. Photograph by John Anglim.

A detail of Carol Goddu's quilt, "Compleat Insanity," is pieced from silks and silkies, then overlaid with black velvet ribbon. Photograph by F. Goddu.

Charlotte Patera combines her trademark reverse appliqué with strip piecing to make a free, casual schoolhouse pattern. Photograph by Charlotte Patera.

Margaret Cusack's machine appliqué raises the technique to the highest levels. Here, "Cat and Daffodils." Photograph by Ron Breland.

This was one of my first "art pieces." Intended to be a rag rug, it became a wall hanging instead on my friends' wall in sunny Colorado. The colors have faded and changed (blue is notorious for that), but it still looks good. Photograph by the author.

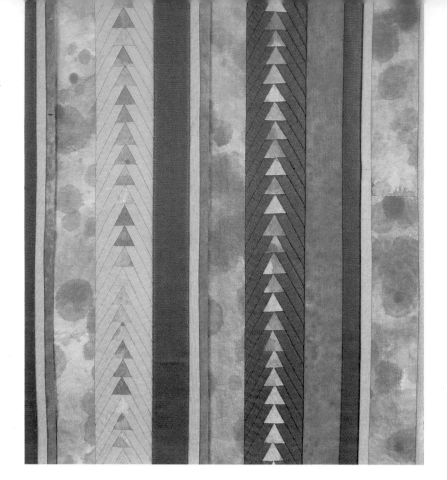

Yvonne Porcella combines Afghani piecework with silk strips. Photograph by Sharon Risedorph.

Hooked rug by Joan Moshimer shows the craft at a high level of sophistication. Photograph courtesy of Rug Hooker News & Views.

SEMINOLE PIECEWORK

FROM SIMPLE TO SPECTACULAR

I'm almost sure it was Robert Rauschenberg who said, in talking about his work, "Sometimes I see it first and then I paint it. Sometimes I paint it first and then see it."

Some bands of Seminole piecework are best worked out carefully for a particular color and style, but it's also a great luxury to have at your disposal several bands of trims you've already stitched together for inspiration. In fact, that's the way the original Seminole skirts and jack-

FIG. 3–1 *These two skirts for little girls are gathered onto elastic for easy fit. Seminole motifs are set on point, then inserted between bands of plain fabric. A skirt like this requires no pattern and can be easily adapted for any length desired. These are designed by Femi Roecker of Bellvale, New York.*

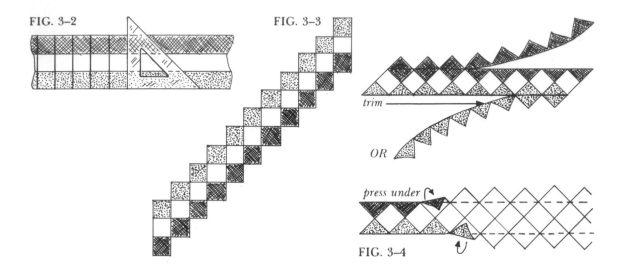

FIG. 3–2

FIG. 3–3

trim

OR

press under

FIG. 3–4

ets were made. The Indian women pre-assembled rectangles of pieced fabric, then chose one for the jacket back, another for the sleeves.

The technique can be quite simple or madly intricate. Perhaps you'll rush right into intricate anyway, but in case you are a rational person, let's begin with simple methods.

Select three strips at least 36 inches long of contrasting color fabrics, all the same length. You can sew different widths of strips together. Width isn't important, but accuracy is; cutting and seaming must be precise.

Sew strips together in ¼-inch seams with a short stitch length (13 to 15 stitches to the inch) and press seams open or to one side. Press toward the darker fabric if that's a choice or toward the lighter weight side if the fabrics naturally fall that way.

Now cut the sewn strip into segments of equal width. Use a square or triangle for this rather than a ruler. It doesn't take any longer, and perfect 90-degree angles will produce prettier finished bands. See Figure 3–2.

Stagger the segments so that each color steps up or down from itself as shown in Figure 3–3. Stitch joining seams, and press to one side. Use your straightedge to mark a continuous line across the top and bottom of the strip, then cut off all the triangle points as shown in Figure 3–4. (Whether you save *them* or not tells us a lot about you.) Sew the diago-

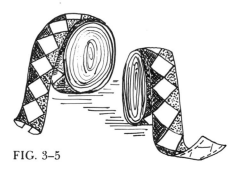

FIG. 3–5

FIG. 3–6 *Seminole piecework lends itself perfectly to clothing and other items made for boys and men. Its clean, geometrical lines complement masculine styles. Here, designer Laura Lee Fritz, of Inverness, California, creates a little boy's vest in which the Seminole segments create a pattern of robots. Photograph by the author.*

nal ends together to make a loop, then cut the loop to make a strip with squared ends.

If you're not ready to use the band, just run a line of staystitching along the cut edges, roll it up and stash it.

Now, select five more strips, narrower this time, and repeat the same stitching, cutting and restitching process. With more strips, narrower strips, colors with more or less contrast, you can see how this same easy method makes dramatically different patterns.

Cutting the segments on the diagonal produces another look, and you can get as fancy as you like.

Because the initial long seams are the speediest ones to sew, make them count. A six-row band is far more spectacular than a three-row band. The second-stage piecing takes most of the time.

SEVERAL WAYS TO USE BANDS

The traditional Seminole Indian costume consists of bands of plain cloth interspersed with bands of piecework and here's where you'll find your madly intricate stuff. Skirts and blousy jackets are made this way. You can use this technique for clothing or household items or art pieces.

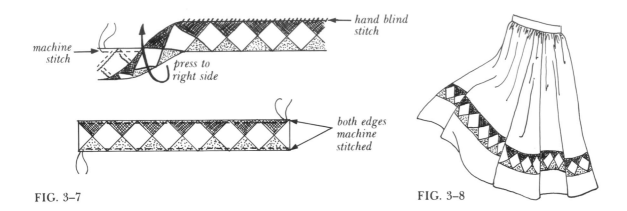

hand blind
stitch

press to
right side

both edges
machine
stitched

FIG. 3–7   FIG. 3–8

You can press under the raw edges and sew the bands to other surfaces. This can be accomplished by machine stitching both long edges
or by machine stitching one edge (right sides facing), then flipping the
band up and blindstitching the second edge in place. See Figure 3–7. If
you elect to use this second method, machine stitch the more visible
edge and hand stitch or machine blind stitch the other. For instance, on
the skirt shown in Figure 3–8, the top edge would be more obvious to
the eye, so it should be machine stitched for a smoother, more uniform
appearance.

QUILTS

In all our discussions of quilts, whether made from strips, bits or trash, whether denim or silk velvet, we'll focus on those that can be made on the sewing machine in a fairly simple, straightforward fashion. One major exception will be crazy quilts, but we can learn some clever timesaving tricks even on these visual wonders.

Too, we won't concern ourselves with purities such as "It isn't a quilt until it's quilted." For our purposes, it's a quilt if it's tied, tacked, machine-quilted, hand-quilted or stapled; if it's a throw, baby cover, wall hanging or art piece.

Check the Suggested Reading for some really good books on quilting in general, scrap quilts in particular.

STRIPED QUILTS

It's quite feasible just to jump into a striped quilt with little or no preconceived notions. When I made "New Bluebird," the challenge was simply to use up all the corduroy scraps. Of course I wanted the quilt to be beautiful, and I also wanted it to be constructed with a minimum of cutting and sewing.

I began with wide strips (4 to 8 inches), piecing occasionally when necessary. This was a major beginning step—easy and quick, and I could then see at a glance the approximate finished size of the piece and what leftover bits I could intersperse between the big solid stripes.

In making quilts, and many other items as well, a big empty wall

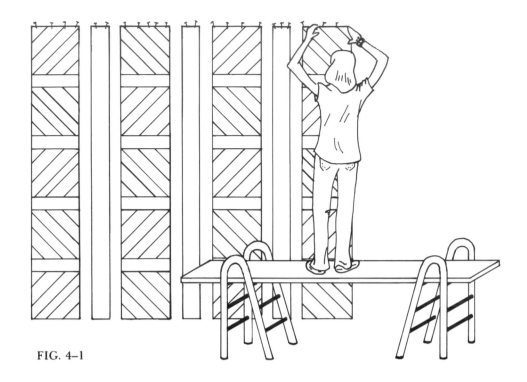

FIG. 4–1

that you can pin or tack into is a major asset. Mine leaves something to be desired (I have to walk barefoot on a bed), but it works.

For fill-in areas between the big stripes, I used quick-square techniques and basic strip piecing. We'll talk more about these in later chapters.

The point is: *You can improvise.* If your fabrics look good together to begin with, and if you leave yourself open to change as the work progresses, you won't go wrong.

Make it easy on yourself. If you find yourself with stripes that look good together, stop right there. The Amish produced stunning quilts consisting of nothing more than vertical stripes, sometimes with a surrounding border, sometimes not.

A note on technique: Even though I cut the pieces for "New Bluebird" meticulously and pieced them together with precision, the finished top had a definite list to starboard. After a quick telephone survey of some of my trusted advisors, I decided this sway was due to the nature of corduroy. As one woman tactfully told me, "Maybe that's why people don't make quilts out of corduroy." Nonsense. Corduroy is

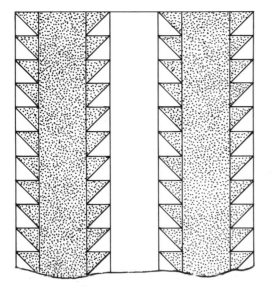

FIG. 4–2

great for quilts because it's soft, snuggly, warm and washable. The answer? A walking foot. I didn't take the quilt top apart (it was scraps, after all), but I did wait until the foot I'd ordered arrived before beginning the assembly and machine quilting. And it helped.

To complete "New Bluebird," I added prairie points (more about them later) and incorporated belt-loop-like strips into the seams to cover the piecing. (Sometimes I get almost compulsive about using up as much of the material on hand as humanly possible. In this case, I took the leftover strips that were too narrow to work into the strip-pieced sections and folded them twice toward the center, then in half—just like you'd make a belt loop—then I double topstitched them. I incorporated these into the seams that joined my long strips together, placing them over piecing seams in the strips. The belt loops cover the seams and add visual interest. Besides, they're fun to run your fingers through.)

ROMAN STRIPE QUILTS

With the Roman stripe pattern, you can make a beautiful quilt fast without sacrificing any subtleties in design. It's an excellent choice for a first quilt and the perfect baby gift for tomorrow's shower. Use two colors, six or twenty.

FIG. 4–3

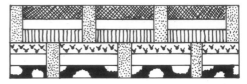

FIG. 4–4

Decide on a workable block size. Just for practice, let's pretend our blocks will all be composed of three strips and that they'll all measure 10 inches square before joining. So cut strips 3½ inches wide and 10, 20, or 30 inches long, in any multiple of 10 or any multiple of the size square you want. It's up to you whether you want to piece the strips to make those increments or not. My main quilting influence was my grandmother. She pieced shamelessly, and sometimes I do too.

Sew the strips together along the long edges, press the seams to one side, and cut into 10-inch-long squares. Sixteen or twenty of those squares are all you'll need for a baby quilt. After you've made enough to create the quilt size you want, make a few extras. This will give you more design options. Arrange the blocks, playing them against each other on the floor or bed or tacking them to a wall. Sew the blocks together in rows, then sew the rows together.

Of course your blocks don't have to be square. You could just as easily assemble rectangles of five narrow strips, sew a perpendicular stripe on the end of each of those chunks and make a basketweave design.

LOG CABIN QUILTS

The log cabin design is incredibly versatile. A log cabin block can be used as a tote bag, vest back, or whatever. You don't have to combine lots of them to make a quilt, though log cabin quilts are visual heavyweights.

FIG. 4–5 *A spin-off from log-cabin quilting designs, these octagonal placemats and coasters are made by surrounding the center square with triangles, then continuing with strips to complete. Designer Ann Wasserman of Evanston, Illinois, stitched through batting and backing fabric to piece and quilt all in one step. Edges are bound with bias to finish.*

In classic blocks, a center square of one color provides a design unity. Traditionally, that square is red to symbolize the hearth of the home, and colors are added to form one diagonal half in a light color, the other in a dark color. Assembling the blocks then becomes a delightful exercise, resulting in countless variations in pattern—courthouse steps, barn raising, streak of lightning. A major exception is the chevron pattern, where all strips are added to two sides of the first square rather than surrounding it. Here is a very simple first course in stitching a classic log cabin block together.

Decide on the width of your strips. For practice, let's say 2 inches wide. Length doesn't matter much. Cut some 4-inch squares, all one color. Divide your 2-inch-wide strips into light and dark piles.

Pick up a short dark strip and sew it to the square. Trim it off even with the square. Next, sew a light strip to the square/strip. Trim it off even, then add another light strip. Work around the center square as far as you like, making symmetrical blocks.

Just as with most quilt designs, you'll have more fun with a few extra blocks for play. It's possible, too, to play with the basic building

FIG. 4–6

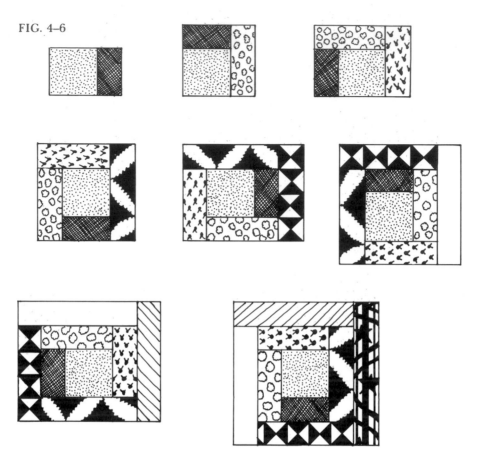

blocks to produce off-center, seemingly curved lines. And it's just as easy. Sew a dark square to a light, then use strips of one width for the dark and strips twice that wide for the light (or vice-versa). For more exaggeration, cut strips with greater differential in width.

Those of you with any hint of math anxiety may have already experienced that exhilarating moment of realizing that these quilts require almost no calculations.

QUICKER CABINS

For even greater speed and efficiency, consider piecing your log cabin blocks right onto squares of bonded batting. It's no trouble, especially if you use a walking foot, and your quilt winds up already quilted.

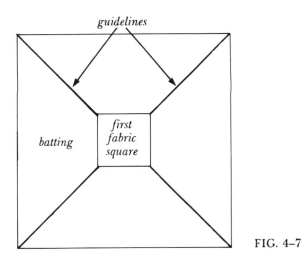

guidelines

batting

first fabric square

FIG. 4–7

After you cut your batting squares, draw lines with a wash-out or fade-away marker, drawing from corner to corner for guides. Place your center square right in the X as shown in Figure 4–7, and sew as usual, except that you'll be sewing through the batting and two layers of fabric.

When you approach the outer edges of your block, leave ½ inch or so unstitched. To assemble the blocks, machine stitch the top fabric only, right sides facing. Trim away excess batting so that it just abuts the next piece. Line the quilt and bind the edges if desired. If you don't want the look of a border that binding produces, you can also sew the lining to the pieced top with right sides facing, leaving an opening for turning. Turn right side out, and slipstitch closed. Tack or tie in a few places just to keep top and lining together. Because of all the machine quilting, of course, the batting will not shift.

STRIP-PIECED BLOCKS

My grandmother, as far as I could ever tell, never threw anything away, would accept anything you wanted to give her, and in turn would give you anything she had. It seemed to work for her, this non-capitalistic system, and now that she is gone, her legacy of scrap quilts remains. She made "Dresden Plate," "Wedding Ring," and other traditional patterns with scraps, but my favorites are her strip-pieced blocks joined with sashing.

I don't know if Ma ever thought about laundering these quilts; I'm sure she didn't prewash or even consider which fabrics she combined. I've seen brand new polyester mixed in with silk from the 40s in her work. Maybe she considered them art pieces—that's how I regard the few that I own.

The beauty (elegance, really) of these quilts is that you can use virtually everything. Longer strips cover the block either straight or diagonally, smaller pieces fill in the corners or add length to an almost-long-enough strip, and trash fabric disappears beneath the strip piecing at a gratifying rate. Ma used her bigger pieces of fabric to make the sashing between the blocks.

Making strip-pieced blocks is the essence of simplicity. Use a square of the proper trash fabric (see Chapter 12 for further discussion) as a base. Cut twenty or so the same size, the number depending on whether you're making a large or a small quilt.

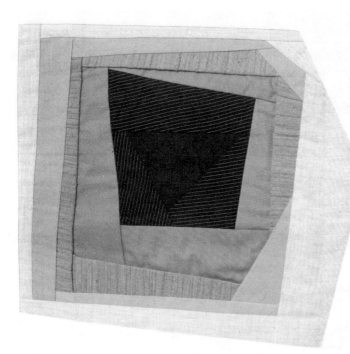

FIG. 4–8 *Lois Ericson of Tahoe City, California, takes the technique of strip-piecing a step further by using varied shapes as well as strips. In this sample, with its illusion of depth, Lois laid down the center triangle, and worked outward, overlapping shapes and strips. Photograph by Jim Fyfe.*

Now just because Ma mixed everything under the Oklahoma sun in her strip-pieced quilts doesn't mean that you should. This is a fantastic way to whip out a baby quilt if you choose washable bright fabrics. (I'd like to know who decided babies like pastels. Studies show they prefer bright, clear colors. And who thought of "saving" baby quilts? The kid should be allowed to use the quilt up, wear it out, wag it around until pitiful tatters fall from it. End of sermonette.)

Whether you opt for practical or frivolous, here's how to do it: Lay your first strip across the base block, right side up. Lay the second strip right side down on the first, with raw edges matching. Machine stitch through all three layers. Here the latitude in technique can be used to your advantage. If your fabrics are sturdy and closely woven, a ¼-inch seam will be fine. If they're more troublesome—slinky or ravelly—use a ½-inch seam. A delight of the strip-pieced block is that consistency can fall by the wayside. Whether you're piecing vertical or diagonal blocks, you can begin at one side or corner, or work from the center outward.

It's up to you whether to finger-press or press with an iron, but however you choose, press the second strip to the right side and lay a third strip on it, again right side down. Only the first strip is applied face up. Sew the third strip down, then continue out to the edges or corners of your block. See Figure 4–9. Don't bother neatening the edges until you're through. I like to machine-baste around the perimeter from the base side when I'm through, then trim the edges to match the base.

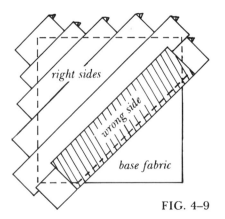

FIG. 4–9

FIG. 4–10

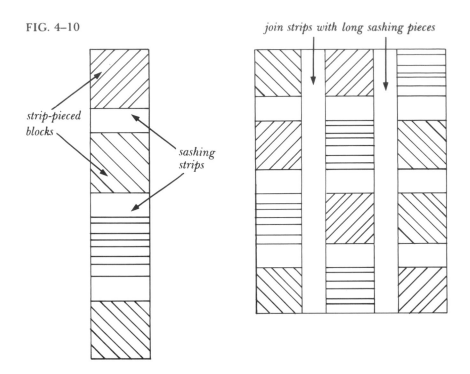

strip-pieced blocks

sashing strips

join strips with long sashing pieces

Decide on the width of your sashing strips, then cut them as long as possible. Take your shorter pieces and join several blocks with them as shown. After you've pieced a strip as long or as wide as you want your finished quilt to be, sew a long sashing strip to it. Now Ma didn't care if all her blocks matched up or not, but yours probably will if all your base squares are identical and if your sashing is even. Another option at this point is to alternate plain with strip-pieced blocks.

Finish however you like. For a spread or hanging, or for warmer climates, you might want to use a cotton sheet blanket inside rather than quilt batting.

WOVEN COVERLETS

These are nifty little items, and they lend themselves well to scrap work. I wouldn't use one for a baby quilt, because they're not very washable, but for a throw or a nap quilt, they're super.

You can line a woven coverlet or not. You do need to decide at the beginning, though, because whether it's lined or not will determine how the strips are constructed. Strips can be as wide or as narrow as you like, but as usual, for practice purposes, we'll make an easy, wide-strip example.

Say you want a nap quilt sixty inches square. Piece lengths of fabric together to achieve lots of strips that length. Strips in a woven coverlet can be varied in width, so if you want to mix widths, go right ahead. At this point, the directions diverge: For an unlined coverlet, machine stitch the long ends right sides facing, using a ¼-inch seam, just as you'd stitch a sash or a strap. Turn to the right side (let your children do this step while they watch Saturday morning cartoons) and press the strips. If you want some really narrow strips in your coverlet, cheat a little. We all know that it's no fun to turn narrow strips, so instead of turning, just fold and sew. Remember, this is a scrap project. You don't want to get bogged down in any step of the work.

For a lined coverlet, just press the strips like you'd press bias tape. See Figure 4–11.

For both methods, it's now time to weave the strips. The only tricky part of this technique is deciding on a workable way to anchor your lengthwise (or first set of) strips. I like to work on a bed, anchoring the first set to one side of the bed with big safety pins. If you can tack or tape

FIG. 4–11   FIG. 4–12

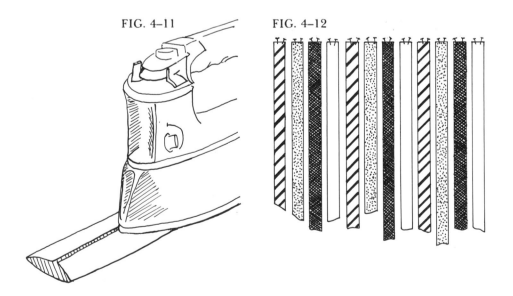

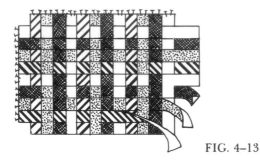

FIG. 4–13

them to the floor or wall without damaging either of those surfaces, that would work, too.

Place the first set of strips with edges just touching, or almost. At any rate, don't overlap them. Now weave the first row of your second set of strips over and under, then the second row under and over. Anchor the ends of these strips as you begin and end the weaving. See Figure 4–13.

Techniques diverge again: For unlined coverlets, staystitch around all the edges to hold strips in place, then bind. Tack here and there to keep strips from shifting excessively.

For lined coverlets, staystitch, then sew to a lining. Tack down at frequent intervals. Remember that your raw edges are merely pressed, not stitched, and you don't want them to show up on the right side of the coverlet ever. Bind the edges.

When you're working on strips for unlined coverlets, it's entirely up to you whether you press with the seam to one side or centered on the back.

COLLAGED CLOTHING

CHANGING THE NAME

So far, we've been free with the word "scraps." This situation changes dramatically when we enter the world of clothing. Gone are the days of hippie patches and Dolly Parton's coat of many colors. Today's fashion scene is far more sophisticated and subtle. To accommodate this trend, we will refer to our clothing as "collaged" rather than made from scraps. Okay? Terminology, however, is our only constriction. Collaged clothing can be as wild as Yvonne Porcella's trademark multi-colored fantasies or as mild as Vickie Senape's ivory strip-pieced jacket (see color section).

WOVEN STRIPS

Accent garments for spring and summer wear with woven strips. The basic technique is the same as for woven coverlets, discussed in the chapter on quilts. Strips for clothing, of course, should be narrower, and the length will be determined by where it's featured in the garment. For wearables, it's a good idea to seam and turn the strips, whether you choose to line the woven area or not.

For a lattice effect, perfect for showing off a summer tan, place unlined strips farther apart than you would for a coverlet. Weave all or part of sleeves, a cut-out section across the back of a blouse, a décolleté yoke. Though this technique is more suited to blouses and jackets, a woven strip down the sides of summer slacks could be appealing.

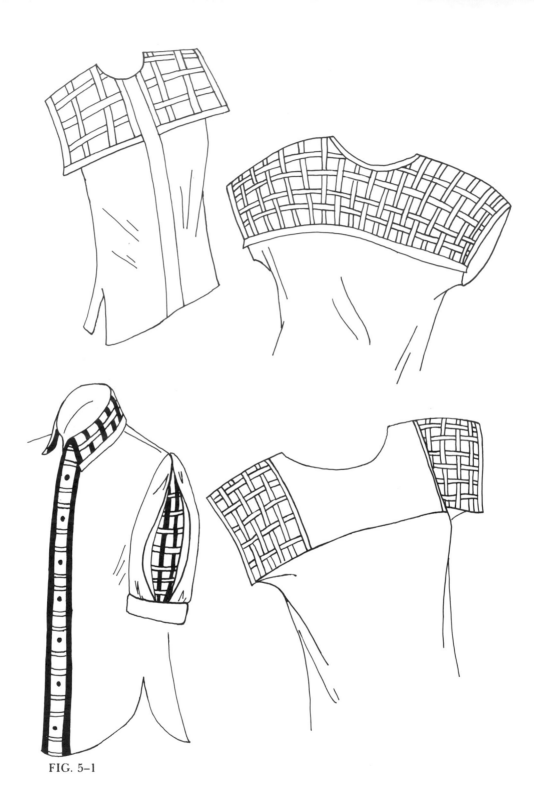

FIG. 5–1

Use unlined strips, too, in garments especially designed to coordinate with the layer below. You could have lattice weaving down the front of a white jacket to be worn over a black sleeveless blouse, for instance. Now if you chose that jacket to wear over a muted floral print, you'd lose all your drama. Choose a contrasting fabric to line woven pockets, cuffs or other accent areas.

STRIP-PIECED CLOTHING

The general technique (and it is *very* general) is discussed in Chapter 4 on strip-pieced quilts, so all we need to talk about here is how making a strip-pieced, collaged wearable differs from making a quilt.

Whereas anything goes in a quilt (after all, it can always become a wall hanging), clothing (darn it all) really does have to fit and enhance the human body. While this narrows our options, it also provides an exciting challenge. As the *I Ching* says, "The great stitcher is strengthened by her limitations." (That's not really true. It actually says, "The great man is strengthened by his limitations." But you get the point.)

Unless a tall person is wearing the clothing, wide strips of various fabrics can be a visual disaster. There are exceptions, but I think strips

FIG. 5–2 *Yvonne Porcella designed this strip-pieced "Vest for All Seasons," planned for scraps of seasonal-print fabrics. Hearts, flags, stars, eggs, and even bones show up here. It's one of those things that makes you smile.*

for clothing should be narrower than for quilts, and of course bulk must be kept to a minimum. Colors may be more subtle if your personal coloring is not dramatic. Choose a lightweight, pliable fabric for your base: light muslin, batiste, old sheet. If you're using trash fabric (see Chapter 12), wash and dry it a couple of times or treat it as you'll clean the garment.

Keep your seams small; trim and grade them. (Grading a seam merely involves trimming one seam allowance a bit narrower than the other so that a ridge doesn't form.) Even though the actual sewing of collaged clothing is every bit as easy as making a strip-pieced quilt, I believe one *must* be more alert in picking up that next strip. (But maybe I'm just too careless with my quilts.)

FABRIC DYE

Don't overlook the collagist's greatest ally—fabric dye. You couldn't dye individual strips, of course, because most household dyes would quite probably fade onto the neighboring fabric, but if you've completed a piece and find that it doesn't quite sing, try dipping the whole shebang into a dye bath. (Upon re-reading this, the words "you couldn't" strike a rebellious chord. Why not? If you're willing to risk the serendipitous blending of colors in the future, try it.) Spinners, weavers and rug hookers frequently use yellow onion skins for this very purpose. If an antique, softening effect would tie the whole project together, simmer about a quart of yellow onion skins in two or three gallons of water for a few hours. (To obtain onion skins, just reach down into the bottom of the grocery store bin beneath the onions. As the skins have a natural tendency to peel off anyway, there's usually a layer of skins several inches thick. Expect an odd look at the checkout counter, but you can handle that).

Strain and cool the solution (extreme heat could shock the fabric fibers). Immerse wet fabric in the dye bath, bring it back to a simmer and hold at that temperature, stirring every ten or fifteen minutes, until it looks a little darker than you want it. Rinse and dry.

Tea can also be used to mute and blend colors and is especially effective to "ivory down" a brilliant white. Color analysts usually tell us to wear no white that's whiter than our teeth. I don't know about your teeth, but most whites are definitely whiter than mine are. Ivory seems to be kinder to skin tones than clear white, too. Use two or three family-size tea bags and steep in two or three gallons of water. Remove bags, cool solution, and proceed as for onion skins.

If you decide that a "real" color would add the cohesion your project needs, use regular household dyes (Cushing is an excellent brand), following the directions for tinting rather than deep-tone dyeing.

AFGHANI PIECEWORK

Before we leave the subject of strip-pieced collaged clothing, let's touch briefly on Afghani piecework. I first saw this pieced pattern in Yvonne Porcella's *A Colorful Book*, and she was kind enough to show me how to do it and give her permission for me to explain her technique to you. Even though I'm not a great hand stitcher, I was sufficiently enchanted by the possibilities to learn how to do it. It's a magnificent portable project, as you can carry all your materials in a cosmetics-size shopping bag. And it goes much more quickly than I'd have guessed. I took enough materials to a seminar to produce two 30-inch strips and finished both in less than three days.

The beauties are: You can do this with your tiniest treasured bits and narrowest strips. You can enlarge the scale if you like. You can sew while traveling or watching television. Best of all, it's just so pretty and mysterious looking that it commands the eye. There's a photograph of a Porcella piece in the color section. I want yards and yards of it in whole rainbows of colors, ready to put anywhere I want.

Here's how: Cut equilateral triangles with sides measuring 2 inches, strips 1 inch wide and 3 inches long. Cut your base strip, to which the triangles and strips will be sewn, as long as you want it and 2 inches wide. The mathematical relation is this: Strips are half as wide as each side of the triangle and 1 inch longer than the width of the backing strip. The backing strip is as wide as one side of the triangle. Thus, if you want 4-inch triangles, you'll use strips 2 inches wide and 5 inches

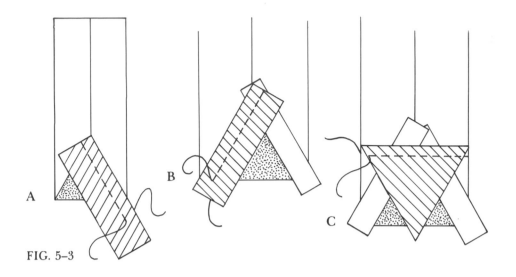

A

B

C

FIG. 5–3

long, all stitched to a backing strip 4 inches wide. That would make a hefty chunk of piecework.

Draw a line up the middle of the strip as a guide to keeping the design straight. Lay a triangle right side up on the bottom of the strip. Lay a strip right side down alongside the triangle, as shown in Figure 5–3A, extending a little way beyond the triangle's top point. Sew in a narrow seam along the length of the strip (A). Finger-press to the right side; follow with another strip on the other side of the triangle (B).

Sew a second triangle, right side down, above the first, testing to see that the base of the second just clears the point of the first (C). Finger-press it up (to the right side) and continue adding strips and triangles until the base strip is covered.

I discovered a little time-saving trick: Sew the first strip (the one on the right side) from the edge of the base strip to the point of the triangle. Without knotting or securing the thread, press the strip to the right side and begin sewing the second strip (down the left side of the triangle.) To minimize the possibility of the piece's curving to one side, alternate the order in which you sew on the strips. For example, let's take two triangles and four strips. Sew the first strip along the right side of the triangle, the second along the left side. After you've stitched the second triangle in place, sew the third strip along the *left* side of it, the fourth along the *right* side. You'll find this method ensures a straighter strip of piecework.

You can do Afghani piecework on the sewing machine if you are a determined machine stitcher, but it's really not the most efficient way if you're working with tiny pieces. I did a sample on the machine with 2½-inch triangles and 1¼-inch-wide strips that was much quicker and neater than had I hand stitched it, but for 1-inch triangles that wouldn't hold true. For slippery, unmanageable fabrics, too, hand sewing would be better and faster in the long run. This is a good airplane project because it's non-threatening. Knitting needles always seem to terrify one's seat neighbors.

You can experiment with different sized triangles, different widths for your strips and different widths for your base strip. One note of caution, though: If your base strip is narrow in proportion to your triangles, you may wind up with a design that looks like Figure 5–4. Now this is a fine design, but it's easy to do by standard piecing techniques — no mystery. For maximum design impact, "float" your triangles by isolating them in the center of the base strip as shown in Figure 5–5 and in the color section.

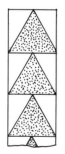

FIG. 5–4

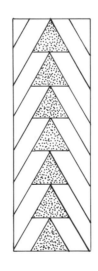

FIG. 5–5

FRINGE WITH LOOSELY WOVEN FABRICS

Here's a way to exploit the very quality that might have induced you to throw loosely woven fabrics into your "trash" container or the charity bin. These fabrics are certainly no good for patchwork, as I learned years ago when I washed "Trip Around the World" quilt and saw all the green squares disintegrate before my eyes. They're not much good for anything in small pieces, except for adding fringe. I took some varied solid colors of coarse cotton/poly fabrics and cut them into strips 2½ inches wide. I wanted long fringe and added the ½ inch for seams. I chose a neutral background fabric in a more sturdy weave and tentatively planned my design.

To start, press a lengthwise, off-center fold in each strip; trim away selvages. The off-center fold makes more fringe actually visible, creating a richer effect. It also produces a smoother finished texture, flowing rather than ridged (like grading a seam). Draw parallel lines on your base fabric close enough so that each row of fringe will overlap the preceding one a half inch or so.

To plan your design, and it should be loose to be true to the medium, just lay your strips out on a flat surface, overlapping them vertically but abutting them horizontally. You can get an accurate size and shape idea from that, though of course the finished piece will be a lot fuzzier.

I laid out my strips to make the biggest piece I could, then cut the backing fabric to match, because I had no earthly idea what I was doing. Would this thing be a pillow, a rug? I have a page torn from an early notebook saying, "Who would want to wear this?"

So I made a big rectangle. I sewed the strips to the base fabric, then pulled threads to make the fringe. I knew one thing—I didn't want *any* of it left over. And there wasn't. I didn't like the rectangle. The fringe looked good only vertically, and rugs and pillows, like cats' fur, tend to get rubbed the wrong way. I kept trying to make it into a practical piece, because it was clearly no art piece. Because I'd been making lots of hippari jackets, I had a note tacked to the wall: "hippari sleeve 22 by 14 inches." My fringed oddity measured 25 by 32 inches. In a flash I cut it in two and make very frivolous sleeves. I'm not sure what else this might be good for, but it's fun. (Shown in color section).

FIG. 5-6

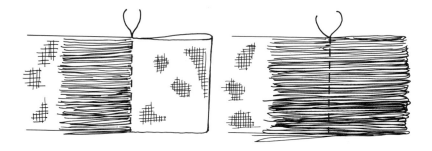

You don't have to stop with straight-edged fringe, either. Trim it in waves, points or random patterns. You might want to consider saving some of the long threads you're pulling out for added design elements. Here's how Loretta Daum Byrne of Cambridge, Wisconsin, handled fringe and leftover threads for a jacket she was making from a luscious

FIG. 5-7

bison/silk handwoven fabric: Along the front edge, she turned the fabric back to the right side and machine stitched it down, just as if she were machine hemming. Then she pulled the threads along the fold as shown in Figure 5–6. This produced a fluffy, loopy, soft effect along the visually important front edges. Then she twisted groups of saved-out threads and tacked them to the bottom edge of the jacket.

You can always fringe sleeve edges and hem edges on loosely woven fabrics. Either leave plain or knot. (Remember all those macrame knots? Now you can use them again.)

Fran Sherwold, of Downey, California, finished one of her beauti-

FIG. 5–8 *B.J. Getchell sews strips to the sleeves of a loosely fitting jacket, uses more strips for waist ties, and adds big Carmen Miranda-style flowers with streamers.*

ful machine-embroidered pullovers by simply turning the front self-facing to the outside, topstitching a quarter-inch from the fold, and fringing the seam allowance. Fabrics that are woven of different threads for the warp and weft (like our old favorite, blue denim) are especially effective fringed in this way.

Robbie Fanning told me about a tunic with self-fringe at the front neckline opening that had been knotted and strung with beads. This causes the front neckline to fall open into a V-shape, although a vertical cut alone has been made into the front bodice. See Figure 5–7.

FABRIC FRINGE

In addition to thread fringe, you can also make fabric fringe. This wonderful stuff just gets better and better with each washing. B. J. Getchell makes fabric fringe creations she calls Raggles; Patty Kreider and Sue Beauford of Artful Illusions (see Sources of Supply) market a pattern for some great wearables made with a similar technique.

Follow the same procedure as if you were making thread fringe; cut the strips, fold under a long edge, and stitch to base fabric. Rather than pulling threads, take your scissors and snip almost to the stitching line, cutting as close to the grain of the fabric as possible. This technique works best with broadcloth-weight 100% cotton fabrics. Patty and Sue advise folding bias strips of fabric to fringe. See Figure 5–9.

Just as in thread fringe, you don't have to stop with a straight cut for fabric fringe. I've seen vests, jackets and clothing accents of zigzagged or pointed fabric fringe. Just cut single layers of fabric as shown in Figure 5–11.

Sew the strip to the basic garment with right sides facing as shown in Figure 5–12. Fold downward and press (see Fig. 5–13). About ½ inch

FIG. 5–9

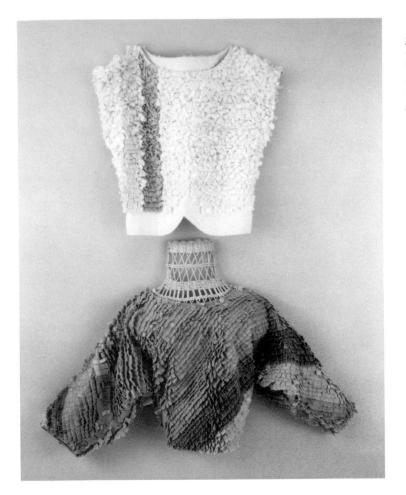

FIG. 5–10 *Artful Illusions, a company composed of Patty Kreider and Sue Beauford, markets patterns for fringed cotton garments. Shown here, sleeveless and three-quarter sleeved pullovers. Photograph courtesy of Artful Illusions.*

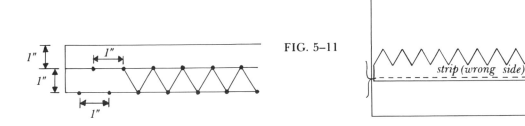

FIG. 5–11

FIG. 5–12

strip (wrong side)

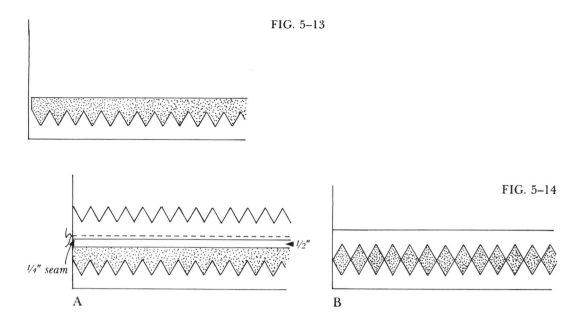

FIG. 5–13

FIG. 5–14

¼" seam

½"

A

B

above the seam, sew another snipped strip (Fig. 5–14A) so that points of the second strip form a diamond shape with the first (B). Continue adding strips until your garment piece is covered.

FABRIC JEWELRY: TUBE BRACELETS AND NECKLACES

I've seen men as well as women wearing these tubes, and one man I questioned about them told me that the tourist-oriented shops in the mountains of Colorado just couldn't keep enough of them in stock. Stuffed tubes make great beach jewelry, too.

Cut a length of fabric on the bias. For a bracelet, measure for a length that will just slip over your hand (no closure). For a necklace that will close, cut the strip to the desired length plus about ½ inch for turning under at the ends. Of course if you want a longer necklace, it will be a continuous loop just like the bracelet. Cut your bias strip wide enough to wrap around cording as thick as you want, plus seams. Be generous—it makes for much easier sewing. Cut your cording twice as long as the bias, plus one inch.

Fold the fabric around the cord, wrong side out. Put a zipper foot or cording foot on your sewing machine and stitch across the cording and the bias strip as shown in Figure 5–16. Stitch down the length of the strip close to the cord, taking care not to catch the cord in the stitching. Note that stitching and fabric begin in the center of the length of cording. (You could also use a length of bulky yarn instead of the cording, as long as the yarn is even in thickness.)

Now pull on the cording, easing the bias strip over the cord to the end. Trim excess cord; save for future use. Butt the ends of cord together for the length desired and sew or dot with glue to hold. Turn ends of strip under a scant ¼ inch and slipstitch together.

If you want a shorter necklace, one that wouldn't slip off and on easily, use Velcro dots or jewelry findings, stitching them to the ends of the tube after you've turned under the ends of the fabric. These tubes are fine to wear just "as is," but they're also a perfect base for fabric medallions, beads, soft-sculptured shapes or other added embellishments.

In addition to smooth tubes, you can make wrinkled ones—suitable not only for jewelry but insertion into or appliqué upon clothing

FIG. 5–15 *Designer Sue Franklin of Wimberley, Texas, uses strips of batiked cotton to make fabric tube jewelry. The top two have batiked circular pendants, while the lower necklace is a simple tube, closed with Velcro.*

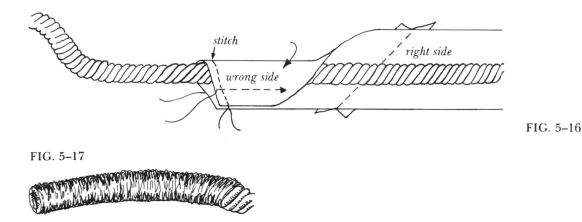

FIG. 5–16

FIG. 5–17

items. Just measure the fabric ½ to ⅓ longer than you'd need for smooth tubing. Follow the same basic steps, then distribute the fullness however you like (see Fig. 5–17). It produces a rich, interesting texture.

ROLLED ROSES

It's easy to make these delicate little confections with scraps of silks and silkies, and you might want to explore the technique more deeply to produce flowers with other fabrics as well.

Take a strip around 12 to 20 inches long and 1 to 3 inches wide. Experiment with straight-grain and bias strips to see which you prefer for different effects. Fold in half lengthwise. You can make a soft roll at this fold by pressing the fabric over a piece of corrugated cardboard or similar material. You can either run a gathering thread along the cut edges of the strip or not. Roll the center part of the rose very tightly and

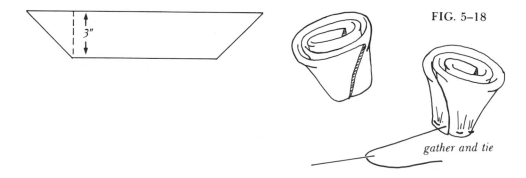

FIG. 5–18

gather and tie

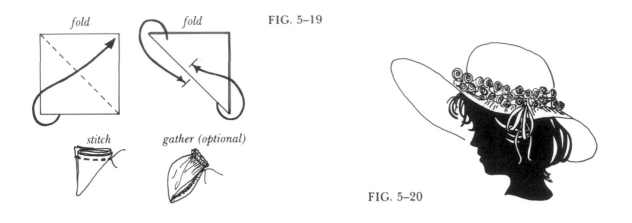

fold   *fold*   FIG. 5–19

stitch   *gather (optional)*

FIG. 5–20

work more loosely toward the outer edges. If you are not using a gathering thread, take several stitches through the base of the rose to secure when you are done. With a gathering thread, it's a simple matter to tighten the threads, wrap the tail around the base a few times, and tie off to secure.

For leaves to accompany your roses, take a square of silk, fold in a triangle, then fold the upper right hand corner over just beyond the center point. Fold lefthand point toward the back, then gather the raw edges. You can also fold both corners to the front for a more stylized leaf shape.

Use these roses on picture frames, lingerie, hats, ceremonial baby garments, or add them to fabric jewelry.

BELTS AND BAGS

Belts are bigger (in both senses of the word) in some fashion seasons than in others, but their cycle is always a short one, and a belt is always a major fashion accessory. Handbags, of course, are standard fare every year, all year 'round, with shapes, materials and colors changing constantly. Both these situations lend themselves beautifully to collaged creations. Whether you create a work of art or a toss-off, you can make stunning belts and handbags by several methods. Let's start with belts.

A simple narrow belt is a perfect way to use a small strip of some precious fabric, be it Ultrasuede, silk velvet or a hand-woven material.

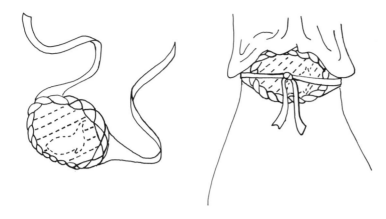

FIG. 5–21

Fabric stores sell belt backing by the yard, and it's a simple matter to cover the backing, add a buckle, and be ready to wear it.

The wrap-and-tie obi belt is a fashion perennial, too. A sandwich of fashion fabric (which for us can be strip-pieced, appliquéd or color-blocked), lightweight interfacing (or use some of your trash fabric), and lining is stitched and turned or bound, and it's ready.

There are times when big, asymmetrical, wide belts are in the fore-front of fashion. Price them in good department stores, note the crafts-manship (or lack of it), and you'll be ready to make your own. The first step is to cut the approximate size and shape you'll want from heavy muslin or interfacing. Remember that your waist/hip area is contoured, not geometrical, so shape accordingly. Use one or several fabrics to cov-

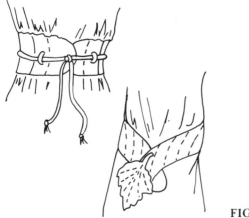

FIG. 5–22

er it. Lois Ericson, one of my favorite belt designers (See Suggested Reading), sews shell slices, antique bracelets and hardware, and all sorts of goodies to her creations.

Don't forget that a good collaged accessory (or any wearable) can be made from different pieces of the same or similar fabrics. There are times when you want flashy, bold contrast, and times when subtle shades of only blue make the statement you desire.

I've heard women say, "I'd wear belts, but I just don't have a waistline." It's true that a good-looking belt will draw the eye to a trim waist, but let me share another visual trick with you. Wear your prettiest belt, toss an open jacket or shirt over it, and voila! The eye is drawn to the waist, cannot measure it, and the mind just assumes that the waist is slender. Try it.

Handbags are easy to copy. As new styles appear in fashion magazines and fancy shops, go over them with an eagle eye and larceny in

FIG. 5–23

mind. I recently saw in an exclusive shop, a pieced Ultrasuede and alligator-print leather bag. The colors (a large mixture of them) didn't really work together, the pieces were machine zigzagged in a rather sloppy fashion, and the price tag was dangerously near $200. It didn't look like a collaged fashion accessory—it looked like scraps. You and I could improve on this bag enormously by discriminating color selection and skillful sewing.

Personally, I love the seasons when huge totes and duffels reign. They don't suit my petite frame at all; I just like them. It's fun to have everything you need for the plane trip, beach, or an overnight stay right there in your bag. These styles are incredibly easy to make. If you wait for a commercial pattern to appear, you might have missed that "fashion wave" you've heard about. You don't want to make your new bag for the season when it's about to become available in the discount stores. Shop in fancy, expensive stores; glance at *Vogue* and *Elle* and other glossy magazines. This doesn't have to cost you a penny. The only admission you pay to get into Neiman-Marcus is the occasional snub by a salesclerk: I can handle that. And your library has those classy magazines.

Tiny evening bags stay pretty much in style forever. Make yours from precious silks, velvets, lamé, shirred organza; decorate it with

FIG. 5–24

FIG. 5–25

beads, rhinestones, shisha mirrors — whatever complements the fabric and your own personal style.

Take any basic handbag shape, duffel, envelope, pouch or whatever, and color-block or strip-piece. Choose a base fabric of sturdy weave and stable fiber content and run with it! Or consider braiding strips to make a clever bag: Hold the ends of three strips securely in place with a C-clamp, office clip, or whatever. For a perfect, neat look, use Braid-Aids (see Sources of Supply) or press edges under as if you were making bias tape. For a ragged, ethnic look, fold the edges in casually as you work or forget about folding them completely.

Once you've braided enough strips, begin sewing them together with sturdy thread. Everyone who has ever braided a rug knows that the darn things buckle and warp anyway, so why not exploit the tendency? Just sew up a round or an oval to the size and shape you want. In sewing the braids together, sew *between* strands of the braid rather than *through* the fabric. In other words, the needle doesn't pierce the fabric, but merely goes under a strand. See Figure 5–25. Add a handle and a lining to complete your braided bag.

RAG KNIT AND CROCHET

Instructions for rag knit and rag crochet sweaters are abundant (see Sources of Supply for a couple of good ones). The most successful of the genre use ½-inch to 1½-inch-wide bias-cut strips, and many will succeed with strip ends just tied together. Rag knitting and crocheting are fast and build the beginner's morale.

Often people who sew well do not knit and crochet. I haven't plumbed the cause-and-effect relationship, but it's there. I'm one of them. It's as if the part of the brain which controls those intricacies has atrophied. Hence, the theory of knitted architectural panels. The theory should hold for crochet, too, though I haven't tested it. Get someone to show you the basic stitches — either knitting and purling or just purling.

The principle is to knit a square or rectangle, then incorporate it into a sewn garment. The panel can become the actual element; sleeves, for instance, or a knitted back for a pieced vest or can be appliquéd over fabric to form a faux architectural panel. This technique is strictly "seat of your pants." Cast on as many stitches as you want, using big needles of course, and knit until you run out of strips or desire.

BRAIDED STRIPS AS CLOTHING ACCENTS

Just as you can use woven strips of fabric for joining, trimming and accenting clothing, you can employ braided strips in much the same manner. Cut not-too-heavy fabrics into not-too-wide strips. Braid neatly, staystitch the ends to secure. Use for yokes, sleeves, or whatever.

BOUND EDGES

It's a great luxury to have pre-cut bindings on hand and to be able to find them. Once you've established the true bias of the fabric, you can fold and cut several layers at a time, producing lengths of bias strips in a flash.

The bias tape makers on the market are wonderful devices that free us from the narrow selection of packaged bias tape—not to mention the economy! See Figure 26A.

Ever on the alert for wider options, we might do well to turn the bias strips into bias tape only when we need it. There are so many other uses for bias strips that it would be a shame to waste the work, only to decide you'd rather use that strip for a Hong Kong seam finish or to make piping. The Hong Kong finish is among the most impressive used in couture sewing for both hems and seams. To make the hem finish, merely machine stitch your bias (strip or tape doesn't matter—you'll soon decide for yourself) to the hem's raw edge, right sides facing. Then turn the bias strip to the wrong side of the fabric, press or pin the hem in place and blindstitch. These steps are shown in Figure 5–26B and C.

For Hong Kong seam finishes, you do the same, except that you catch stitch the second bias edge to the underside of the seam allowance. This is a marvelous finish for unlined jackets or skirts.

If you're unaccustomed to hand-finished seams (or beading or hand appliqué or any handwork), try to incorporate them into your repertoire. Until I took a workshop with Ann Hyde and her talented in-

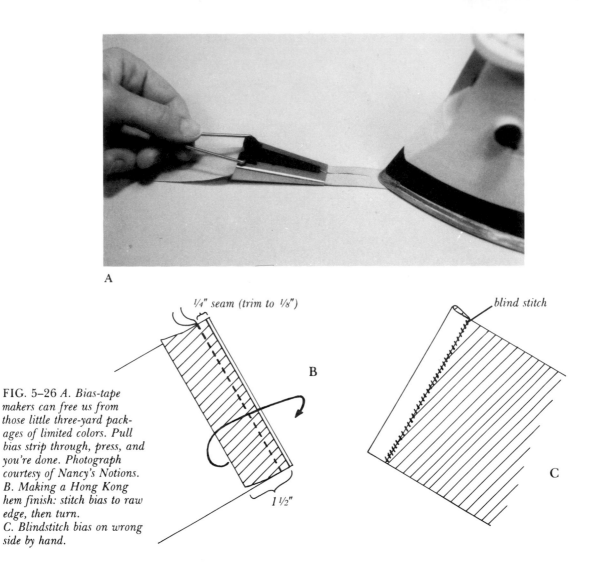

A

¼" seam (trim to ⅛")

B

blind stitch

1 ½"

C

FIG. 5–26 *A. Bias-tape makers can free us from those little three-yard packages of limited colors. Pull bias strip through, press, and you're done. Photograph courtesy of Nancy's Notions. B. Making a Hong Kong hem finish: stitch bias to raw edge, then turn. C. Blindstitch bias on wrong side by hand.*

structor Mary Roby, I would sew by hand only reluctantly. In the haute couture sewing workshop, of course, hand sewing was demanded and chairs were set up on a balcony overlooking a village in the Rocky Mountains! We found ourselves prolonging that hand sewing time when we could alternately bask in the warm sun and watch black clouds pouring over the peaks. Now that I've had that charmed orientation, I rather look forward to handwork and save it for special times.

This section could easily be subtitled "A Love Song for Lois Ericson." I first discovered Lois through her books, which are listed in Suggested Reading. I was instantly captivated by her boundless imagination and vast knowledge of techniques, many drawn from far-flung ethnic wellsprings. Just as inspiring as Lois's words and ideas are Diane Ericson Frode's "tell the story at a glance" line drawings. My favorite of the books remains *Design & Sew it Yourself*, in which Lois shares a generous collection of ideas on button loops and buttons. I learned the basics

FIG. 5–27

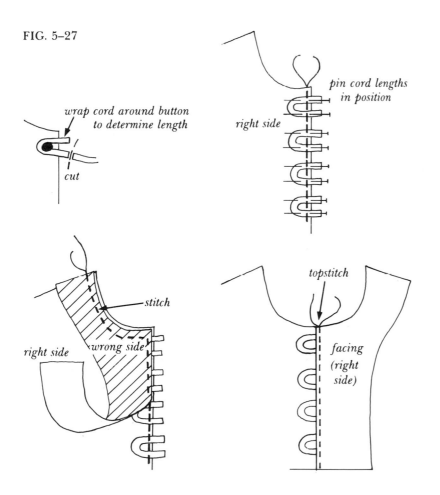

(which follow) from her pages, but countless variations await the interested reader.

Start with a length of cord or yarn twice as long and a bias strip three times as wide as your perfect imaginary finished cording. Use a zipper foot to stitch the bias strip around the cord as shown in Figure 5–16. Trim, then pull. Cut off the excess cord. Ann Hyde taught us this same method in her haute couture sewing workshop, so it must be widely known. Until I learned it, though, I used a method that involved some cursing. So there you have perfect finished cording. You'll find a thousand uses for it. For now, let's limit ourselves to closures.

Incorporate loops of cording as you sew on facings for self-fabric or high-contrast button loops. Edge-stitch the facing to keep the loops lying flat. See Figure 5–27. Lois also suggests hand sewing a long length of cording to the finished edge of a garment, leaving the cording unstitched in some areas just enough to allow a button to slip through.

For knot buttons, take a length of cording about ¼ inch in diameter and 8 inches long. Make a figure "6" with the short tail on top. Make another loop behind the 6, then loop the long end of the second loop over the tail of the 6. Follow Figure 5–28 to finish weaving the long tail

FIG. 5–28

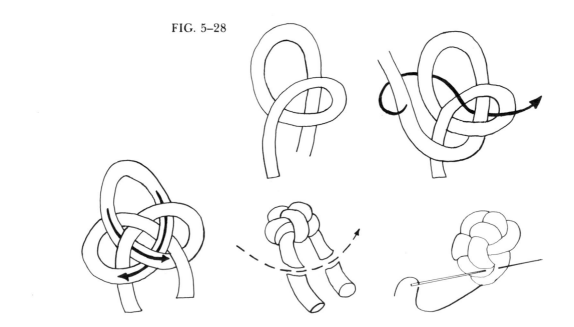

under, over and under. Tighten the ends, pulling the two center loops in the direction of the arrows, then easing the loops closed. Working slowly enables you to shape a perfectly round ball. Cut the cording ¾ inch from the end and sew the ends together. Tuck sewn ends inside the ball and stitch. Leave your threaded needle on the end; sew immediately in place.

To make frogs, begin with a knot button with a 2-inch tail (Fig. 5–29A). It will take about 1½ yards of cording to make a set of two frogs, one with button, one with loop. Follow Figure 5–29 to create these simple, classic frogs, blindstitching each one to garment edge and tacking to secure each loop as it's laid in place (B, C); D shows the matching loop on other side of closure.

Lois goes on to give step-by-step directions for ornate frog designs as well as sources of frog inspiration: Celtic jewelry, nautical books showing knots, and nature photography.

FIG. 5–29

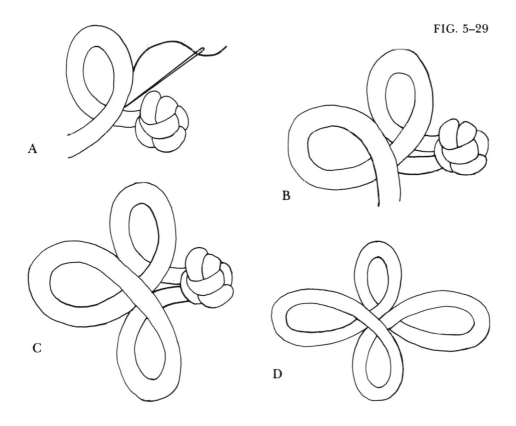

CAMISOLES

Consider the camisole as a major fashion weapon. Where I live, in hot north-central Texas, the camisole has achieved the status of a fashion necessity, but 100-degree temperatures aside, the benefits of this garment are many. You can wear one under a jacket or open shirt to color-coordinate a tailored or glamorous look without the bulk of a blouse. You can wear one under a blouse or dress that's just a little too low-cut for comfort. Have you ever gone to an important meeting in a hotel conference room and found yourself freezing or perspiring? The comfort quotient of a camisole paired with a long-sleeved jacket is insurance not to be disdained.

The camisole in its purest form fits squarely into our subject, because most sizes require only ½ yard or so to complete. Take a half-yard of fabric (36 inches wide will work for size small; 45 inches is needed for medium or large) and fold as shown in Figure 5–30. Cut top at an angle so that the back will be slightly lower than the front. Sew center back seam. You can either make a narrow casing for elastic around the top or

FIG. 5–31

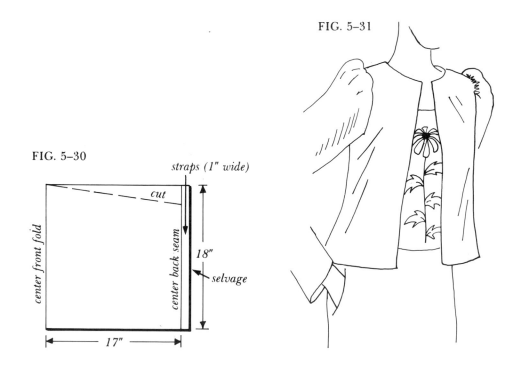

FIG. 5–30

just slightly gather the front to the fullness you need. If you cut facings for the top front and back edges, you can insert straps invisibly within the facing seam. Of course you can just hem the top edge and sew straps in place, too. Add to all this versatility the fact that you can collage the camisole, and you're reckoning with a major factor.

You can strip piece a camisole, but only with lightweight, drapable fabrics stitched to an equally lightweight base fabric. Silks, rayon challis, batiste, would all lend themselves to this method and produce a flattering and comfortable garment.

Think about using the braided strips to make straps for your camisole. What better use for a 4-inch-wide strip of precious brocade or embroidered fabric than to stitch it into the front panel of a camisole? Worn with the right cover-up, it can create the illusion that the entire garment is made from that fabric. And of course you'll combine it so cleverly with the adjacent fabrics that even with the jacket off, it'll be beautiful.

MEADOW POINTS

Like so much of the material in this book, the placing of meadow points in the clothing section is purely arbitrary. Like their first cousins, prairie points (see Chapters 10 and 11 for a discussion of prairie points as clothing, rugs or quilts), could be used in any number of ways. They're fine for clothing, though, so here they are. I learned about them from Nancy Zieman, and the technique is given here with permission of Joan Padgett of Tomorrow's Heirlooms (see Sources of Supply).

Cut strips as long as you need to cover or trim the item you're making: let's pretend it's a skirt. You'd cut several strips as long as the width of your skirt and 2 inches wide. Use fabrics that do not fray readily, as this technique involves snipping and hand-stitching. Fold the strips in half lengthwise with the wrong sides facing and press. Cut 1¼-inch-wide strips from your skirt fabric to place between the meadow-point strips.

Lay a folded meadow-point strip on the right side of a plain strip, matching the raw edges, as shown in Figure 5–32. Notice that the meadow-point strip is folded, while the plain strip is of a single thick-

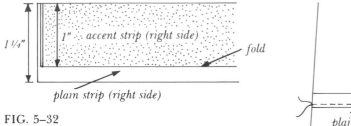

FIG. 5–32

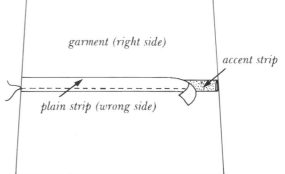

FIG. 5–33

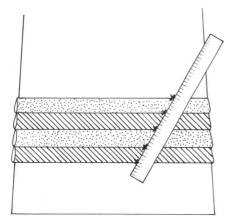

FIG. 5–34

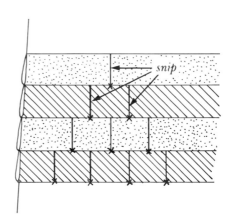

FIG. 5–35

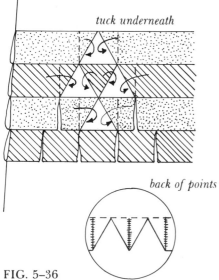

FIG. 5–36

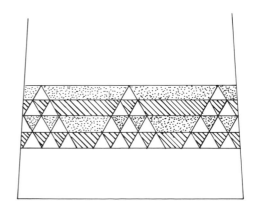

FIG. 5–37

ness. Pin. Place this assemblage on the skirt, right sides facing. The meadow-point strip will be sandwiched between the plain strip and the garment (see Fig. 5–33). Sew through all thicknesses in a ¼-inch seam; press. Continue adding plain and accent strips. Start with three or four; later you might decide to cover a surface with meadow points.

Now lay a ruler diagonally across the strips and mark each one where the ruler intersects it. See Figure 5–34. Snip the folded meadow-point strips through both thicknesses of fabric all the way to the seam at each mark as shown in Figure 5–35. Fold each snip under to form an inverted V. Hand stitch each section of snipped fabric together as shown in Figure 5–36. Snip on whatever marks you like to create geo-metrical designs of your own choice. Figure 5–37 shows how this four-band design might turn out.

RUGS

SHAGGY RUGS ON HAIRPIN LACE LOOMS

A hairpin lace loom can be just a piece of coathanger wire bent back on itself to form a long loop or a thoughtfully designed, table-mounted permanent tool. The simpler versions are fine for their original purpose of making yarn loops for doll hair, animal fur, wigs, or whatever. When taken out of their realm of yarn, though, these lightweights might be unwieldy. I used a sophisticated version (the Shaggy Spinner—see Sources of Supply) to make a shaggy rug from fabric strips.

Of course you know the principle of the hairpin lace loom: You wrap yarn (or fabric strips here) around two parallel bars, stitch down the middle (Fig. 6–1), and slide the loops off the bars. Then you can either cut the loops or not.

For a shaggy rug, you can use or combine straight and bias, torn and cut, wide and narrow strips. You could even wind and include some yarn in with the fabrics. After converting this yarn technique to fabric strips, the only part of the process I'm still not happy with is joining the strip ends. Fool-proof but too time-consuming for me is overlapping diagonally cut ends and running a line of machine stitching through them. Fast and pretty is just tying the ends together in overhand knots. The drawback? If a knot winds up where the loops are to be machine stitched to the backing fabric, you probably won't be able to sew through it. You can just break your stitching and begin on the other side of the knot, but that's not quite perfect either. Maybe you'll come up with the perfect solution. In the meantime, it's still a marvelous method of making a fine rug.

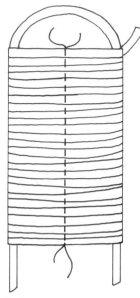

FIG. 6–1

After you've wound as many strips onto the bars as your hairpin lace loom will hold, sit down at the machine and sew the loops to a strong backing fabric. (Excellent use for tough but ugly trash fabrics.) Begin stitching from the open end of the loom, using a size 16–20 (European size 100–120) needle and sturdy thread, and just sew right down the middle of the loom. Pull the bars out when you've finished stitching, wind some more strips, and repeat the sewing process. Because of the nature of the rug (or chair seat or whatever you make out of this fluffy stuff), these many joinings become invisible. If you've hemmed or bound the raw edges of your backing fabric, you're finished as soon as you've covered its surface. Because this method can distort the backing, though, you might want to try sewing on the strips and then cutting the backing to match that.

Shaggy rugs use up tons of fabric, both strips and trash, and are marvelous cuddly things to have around your house.

PLEATED PETAL RUGS

These rugs are very frilly and feminine. I can't conjure one up in rust and gold, but floral colors come freely to mind.

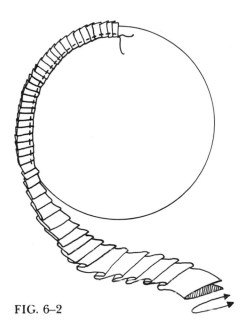

FIG. 6–2

Start with a circle of trash fabric the approximate size of your finished rug. Hem or bind the edges; mark the center. If you have a pleating attachment on your sewing machine, use it to pleat strips about 5 inches wide as shown in Figure 6–2. If you don't have a pleater, just gather the strips. For gathering this much fabric, use the zigzag-stitch-over-string method rather than long machine basting.

Sew the first strip onto the base around the outside of the circle with the fold of the ruffle covering the backing. Sew the second strip with the fold covering the stitching of the first strip. Continue sewing concentric circles of colors toward the center, then machine appliqué a center circle to cover the last line of stitches.

EASY WOVEN RAG RUGS

What's all the fuss about weaving? Sure, you can buy twelve-harness looms that wouldn't even fit into your living room, monsters that might demand the next five years of your life to master. But weaving can be so easy, so pleasant, so available.

Some fabric lovers push their materialistic passion to the limits. I did. Sewing and collecting were not enough. I wanted to learn to weave as well. And circumstances took care of that, as so often happens. (Just as there are no mistakes in sewing, only design opportunities, so are there no accidents in life.)

I happened to be at a birthday party where the honoree was given a good little English table loom as a present — luckily by someone not at the party. My friend opened the box and said rather scornfully, "I'll never do this. Do you want it?" *Did* I? I was living in a 100-year-old adobe in the mountains of northern New Mexico. I had electricity for my major luxury, but no running water and certainly no extra money. The loom and I became inseparable. I wove everything that would hold still and some things that struggled. I unraveled sweaters and re-wove the yarn, leaving the curly edges as designer touches. I cut up every cast-off fabric bit I could find for experimentation.

I found that I could weave table runners, bags and placemats on my little table loom, using rag strips cut or torn no wider than one inch. But I wanted bigger, stronger, heavier, *realer*. I was ready for a rug.

I know lots of women who think nothing of building shelves, replacing spark plugs and mending the roof. I admire them and aim for that status myself some day. But I asked my husband if he'd knock together some two-by-fours for my first rug loom. He did, and it was a primitive wooden frame, braced with plywood triangles at the corners, and big enough to weave a two-by-three foot rug. I hammered nails into the top and bottom and stretched the warp threads around them.

I leaned the frame at an angle against the wall, sat on a pillow on the floor, and sank into the joy of rug weaving. My first discovery was that this style of weaving evoked ancient memories. I could have been an Anasazi woman in pre-Arizona, a nomad stopping briefly in a yurt in the desert. As the weaving progressed, I added cushions and then a stool to raise me to the right level.

A 2- by 3-foot rag rug uses up a lot of fabric, and it doesn't really take that long. I made half a dozen rag rugs on my rough frame before I began lusting after a traditional Navajo loom and asked my husband and son to put it together for me. This loom is far more serviceable, free standing, and a real joy to use.

Weaving is so simple. Once the lengthwise threads are stretched tightly, you can weave in the rag strips with your fingers or a big wood-

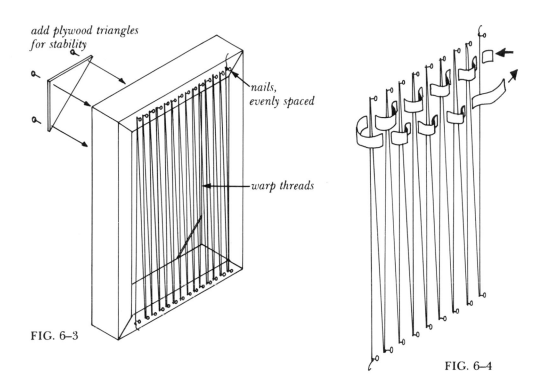

add plywood triangles for stability

nails, evenly spaced

warp threads

FIG. 6–3

FIG. 6–4

en needle with a large eye. Overlap strips an inch or so where they join, and beat each row of weaving down compactly against the preceding row. For the beating, you can use a dog comb, your fingers, or a big cooking fork. An Afghan nomad might use the flat side of a sword. A real beater only costs $8 or $10 and is worth it.

After the rug is woven, you just cut the warp threads, tie them in knots to secure the weaving, and you're done.

In addition to random stripes, you can actually weave pictures with rag strips.

Caution: Rag rugs, even non-pictorial ones, often turn into art pieces.

HOOKED RUGS

Hooked rugs can be any size or shape, painterly or primitive. Their value appreciates with age, and a well-made hooked rug endureth forever. The process is simple—strips of fabric cut on the straight grain are pulled up through burlap to form loops. The density of the packed loops stabilizes the piece. Loops can be low or high, left looped or sheared.

The *art* of hooking rugs, once the technique of even hooking is mastered and the design selected, lies in dyeing the fabric. We'll just gloss over that, knowing that if you get hooked on this technique and enjoy hooking "as-is" strips, you'll scout out that information for yourself. *The Complete Rug Hooker*, by Joan Moshimer, is probably the best book on the subject, and it's listed in Suggested Reading.

To practice, stretch a piece of burlap tightly in a frame or hoop and mark your design on it. The hook is similar to a crochet hook set into a wooden handle. Now your serious rug hookers work with strips ⅛ inch wide or narrower (!) cut from 100% wool. This produces a smooth finished texture and allows for the intricate shading so typical of the best hooked rugs. You may become a serious hooker some day, and more power to you. For practicing, though, use whatever sturdy woven fabric

FIG. 6–5 *Betty Whitwell of Guilford, Connecticut, shows an example of primitive hooking, worked on coarse burlap with hand-cut strips. Note the uneven texture and the rough look.*

FIG. 6–6 *A more polished, traditional style of hooking is shown here worked by Betty Whitwell. Machine-cut strips of woolen flannel are hooked into fine, even burlap.*

FIG. 6–7 *Just because it's hooked doesn't mean it has to be a rug. Mary Seigfreid makes hooking accessible with her small projects (see Suggested Reading). Here are four hooked belts. Fastened at the back and showing under a jacket—instant folkloric chic!*

comes to hand. Cut it on the straight of the goods and about ¼ inch wide or slightly less.

Hold the fabric strip underneath the hoop with your left hand. Pull one end of the strip through the burlap with the hook (see Fig. 6–8A). Insert the hook a thread or two away (this depends on the burlap and the width of the strip) and draw up a loop (B). Continue drawing up loops, leaving the end of the strip as well as the beginning extending up to the right side of the design (C). Later you can trim them even with the loops, and they'll disappear. Pack the loops densely but without distorting the backing fabric, not too tight but not too loose. The loops should comfortably touch each other. The tension created in the backing fabric holds the loops securely in place.

I recently saw in a gallery the hooked art of Leslie Kuter, a woman from Washington. The first piece that caught my eye was a head of Rembrandt, about life size, worked in deep, beguiling, subtle tones. The piece was head-shaped, neatly finished around the edges. Another of the works showed an old-fashioned golfer at the beginning of his swing. It was almost photographic, with rich shading and fine detail. The panel was a good five feet tall by three feet wide. Art *can* be created from unexpected materials.

FIG. 6–8

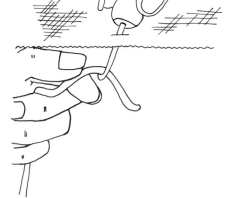

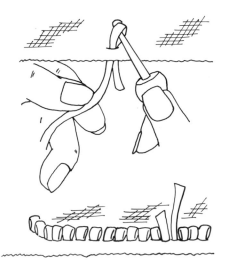

A

B

C

The only difficult thing about braiding rugs is working around the curves so that the rug lies flat. This is achieved in the lacing process by judicious skipping of strands to allow slack. In other words, while you'd catch every strand of the inner braid, you'd lace into perhaps every other strand of the outer braid as it curves around the smaller, inner braid. How many strands you catch and how many you skip depends largely on your fabric and rug shape. Other than that, there's nothing to it.

Cut or tear fabric strips (again, the purists use only 100% wool) into strips around 2 inches wide. Fold (press, too, if you want) like single-fold bias tape, then braid three strands together. There are devices on the market (see Sources of Supply) to make the folding process more streamlined.

Once the strands are braided, you lace them together with sturdy thread (linen is good) and a darning needle. There's an illustration of this step in Chapter 5 on Belts and Bags. Braided rugs can be round, oval, rectangular or even novelty shapes. One or more rows of braiding were sometimes used as borders for hooked rugs.

FIG. 6–9

POKED MATS

Except for the time-consuming chore of coming up with hundreds of 1-by 2-inch snips of fabric, this technique seems to be the easiest way to produce a rug in the field of scrap craft. I read about it in a magazine called the *Canadian Guider* (October 1984). Monica Frim's excellent article tells how an 87-year old resident of Grand Bank, Newfoundland, Louise Belbin, makes these mats.

The only tool you need is a 5-inch length of dowel rod or broom handle whittled to a point and smoothed. Stretch the burlap backing in a frame or hoop (see Fig. 6–10), draw your design onto it, and (working from the back) just poke the ends of each fabric strip through holes in the burlap mesh about ½ inch apart. No knots are tied. When the poking nears the outer edges of the burlap, remove the rug from the frame, turn the edges under, and finish the poking through double layers. In this way, no binding will be needed, as a finished edge will be produced. In the alternative, you can sew on a binding and tack it to the mat's un-

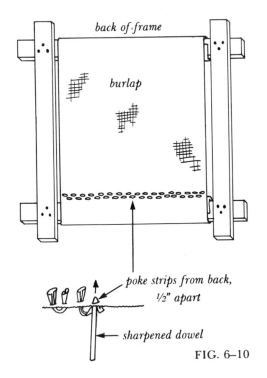

back of frame

burlap

poke strips from back, ½" apart

sharpened dowel

FIG. 6–10

Visualize cross-stitch embroidery worked on even-weave fabric. Now magnify it several times, and you've got the picture. Some needlework techniques appeal to us because of the finished effect. For instance, I think smocking is lovely, beautiful stuff, but I have no desire to take pleater and needle in hand and actually do it. Other techniques cry out to be experienced, for the process as much as for the product. Such a technique, for me anyway, is stitching rugs on canvas with fabric strips. The first time I saw such a rug, I wanted to make one.

Suzanne McNeill calls her version of this craft Rugpoint and shares her method here. Work on a base of 3.3 rug canvas. Cut or tear strips of cotton or cut poly/cotton blend fabrics 1 inch wide. Thread end of strip into a large (grospoint or Rugpoint) needle and work diagonal continental stitches just as you'd follow a cross-stitch chart. Keep your stitches very loose. After you've worked a color area across one row, turn the canvas upside-down and work the second row, turn it again, etc. If the canvas distorts while you work, lay wet press cloths on it and press with

FIG. 6–11 *Suzanne McNeill, of Design Originals, works continental stitch on rug canvas with fabric strips. You can adapt cross-stitch or needlepoint charts to use with this technique. Long-lasting, heirloom results are easy, and do these rugs ever use up the scraps!*

a hot iron from both sides. This makes it flexible enough to stretch and shape back into a perfect rectangle.

Fold canvas edges under and work stitches through both layers of canvas to finish the edges or you can bind, and then turn binding to the underside and stitch to the canvas.

KNOTTED COILED RUGS

Easy enough for children to make, picturesque enough for the choosiest interior designer, these knotted and coiled rugs are great. Each washing makes them fluffier and more welcoming to chilly or shower-wet toes.

Though you can use almost any sturdy fabric, the technique lends itself well to knits because of their propensity to roll. I've seen them made of stiff, unwashed, new calico, however, and they still work. Double a length of clothesline cord or similar cord. You'll soon learn how long a piece you can conveniently handle, perhaps two yards. Secure the ends for greater speed. Use C-clamps to clamp them to furniture, trees, whatever. Cut your fabric strips into lengths of around 5 inches; widths may vary. Knot ends of cord (Fig. 6–12A). Knot each strip onto the doubled cord as shown in B. (Can you stand any more weaving education? All right, this is the rya or Ghiordes knot.) Keep knotting. When you just can't wait any longer to see how your rug will look, take some heavy thread and a big needle and begin sewing into a coil, working from the smooth side. When you run out of cord, tie on a new length as shown in Figure 6–13A.

FIG. 6–12

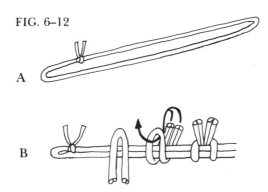

A

B

FIG. 6–13

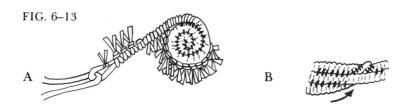

To finish, tuck the last end in, then sew it in place, as shown at B. Trim the pile to a reasonably flat surface and enjoy!

MORE RUGS

Just as you can knit and crochet sweaters and other wearables, substituting fabric strips for yarn, so can you produce sturdy and beautiful rugs with these methods.

Nothing adds warmth, charm and high touch like a handmade rug on the floor. From our grandmother's catch-as-catch-can random patterning to sleek, well-thought-out color blocks, the knitted or crocheted rug can become a major statement in our homes' decor. And if you're one of those productive/compulsive people who can scarcely stand to

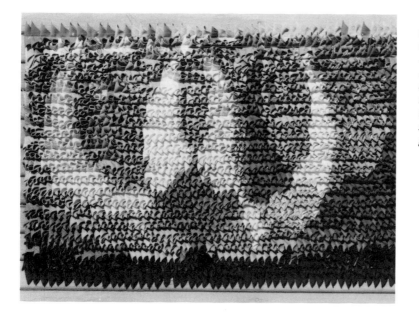

FIG. 6–14 *This cozy, beautiful and ultra-simple rug was made by Gunnar Sundstrom of Palm Bay, Florida. He sewed squares of double-knit fabric folded into triangles onto a heavy backing. It's easily washable and should last forever. Photograph by the author.*

watch television without some handwork, you'll find rug crocheting or knitting ideal. It requires little attention, except for the important form-and-function detail that a rug must lie flat.

According to Phyllis Hause, purveyor of Aunt Philly's Toothbrush Rugs, this easy method of rugmaking has been around for years. At a recent national needlecraft show, however, her booth was constantly crowded with people craning their collective necks to see her work easy half-hitches with one fabric strip around a core of another strip — with a tool made from an old toothbrush. The toothbrush rugs are worked with strips cut or torn into 2-inch widths. You'll find more information in Sources of Supply.

HOUSEHOLD ACCESSORIES

RE-WOVEN CHAIR SEATS

So the old cane or rush seat finally fell out of your favorite porch-sitting chair. Whether you want to keep using an heirloom while you search for a craftsperson to repair it properly, or just prolong the life of a flea-market bargain, consider re-weaving a seat from fabric strips.

Use some of your longer, wider and sturdier strips for this project. Begin at the back left-hand corner of the chair and seat-to-be. Tie a strip end to the back (or hand-sew the strip on) and wrap it around and and around the chair seat from front to back and back again. Wrap the strips closely and let them roll or wrinkle as the succeeding strips crowd against each other. Tie on additional lengths as you need them. If the knots prove uncomfortable to sit on, it's a simple matter to poke them through to the back.

Tie off to secure the front-to-back strips. Tie on a new length of strip, again at the back left-hand corner, but this time tying the strip end to the side of the chair. Weave these crosswise strips over and under the chair sides. Continue weaving back and forth until you've filled in all the open area, or as much as you want to, then tie the last strip to the chair side.

Instead of using the strips flat for making seats, you can use wider strips twisted tightly. This produces a corded or reed look and is very strong. Use the same over-and-under technique or follow the old traditional pattern for rush weaving. Check Sources of Supply for a booklet on traditional rush and cane weaving.

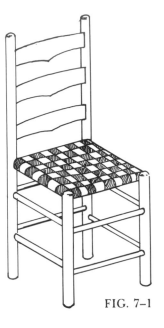

FIG. 7–1

BEADED GARLANDS

Although they look like individually stuffed little fabric balls that would take hours to make, they're really quick and easy. Make them small and precious and wear as jewelry, or make them huge for decking the tree at Christmastime.

Sew and turn a tube; sew or pin one end closed. Stuff a ball of fiberfill into the tube, then thread on a bead. Follow with another ball of stuffing, another bead. Use silk or silkies and glass beads, broadcloth and wooden beads. The only tricky part is getting the end of the fabric tube through the hole in the bead. Of course you'll choose beads with big holes. Staystitching the end of the strip before joining it into a tube helps, so does fabric stiffener. Depending on the fabric and the bead, too, you can roll the end of the tube diagonally around the seam with just a flick of your finger and thread it through.

It's simple to add more length to the tube, so work with easy short lengths for speed in stuffing. When the first tube is filled, machine stitch the end of a second to it, then add a bead to cover the seam. To close the tube into a loop, add a bead, then hand stitch the ends together and

FIG. 7–2

ease the bead over the seam (see Fig. 7–2). Make sure your circle is the desired size before joining the length with that last bead.

PLACEMATS AND HOT PADS

Remember those potholders we used to weave on little plastic frames in elementary school? The only thing lacking in those potholders was our weaving material—rayon or polyester strips. Take the same technique, substitute some silk and velvet strips, and create a magnificent table mat. Or make a set of cotton placemats and a hot pad for the table.

Use almost any rectangular frame for your loom—a picture frame, window frame, a dresser drawer. It's up to you if you want to drive small nails into the ends to space your warp threads. You might try one mat without the nails, then one with them. (There's more likelihood of creating an art piece without the nails.)

The lengthwise threads, or warps, have some stress on them dur-

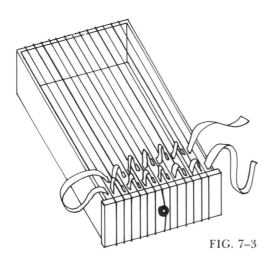

FIG. 7–3

ing the weaving process, so pull on them to test for strength. Perle cotton, household twine or kite string all make good mat warps.

We talked about the basics of weaving in Chapter 6 on rugs; weaving a mat is exactly the same but easier. Use finer, narrower strips, mixing thick and thin, matte and shiny. Tie one new strip to the end of the last, or overlap strips an inch or so to join. When the piece reaches the desired size, cut it loose from the frame. Zigzag stitch the ends or tie into fringe. You can also use such a woven piece to upholster a chair seat, bench or footstool.

STICK WEAVING

You can buy weaving sticks (see Sources of Supply) or make your own. Each stick is nothing more than a wooden needle, through which yarn is threaded. The commercial ones on the market now, sold in sets of five for approximately $5.00, are about ¼ inch in diameter and about 6 inches long. Use any number of them (or as many as you can conveniently handle) to weave bands of almost any length desired. The bands

FIG. 7–4 *Weaving sticks are a simple way to create bands and straps. Traditionally they're used with yarn, as shown here, but it's possible to weave with some fabric strips as well. Try T-shirt knits, silks and similar lightweight fabrics. Don't stop with the bands. You can zigzag stitch them together to make other things. Photograph courtesy Kleids Enterprises.*

can then serve as straps, handles, or the like, or you can zigzag stitch them together on the sewing machine to form baskets, bags or any number of flat items. The strips, in other words, become modules for further sewing.

Thread a length of yarn through the eye of each stick and pull it through until the ends are even, producing a doubled length of yarn. Knot the ends together. Hold two to five sticks in your hand as shown in Figure 7–5. Begin weaving by bringing a length of yarn up from underneath near the middle of the sticks and leaving a 4- to 6-inch tail beneath. Weave over and under to the top stick (the one farthest from you), then under and over to the bottom stick, then back. That's basically it. As the sticks fill up, pull them to the right a little, always leaving some of the weaving on the sticks. When you want to add a new strip of yarn or change colors, leave the "tail" hanging out toward you, and come up from the back side again. You can take care of the tails when the weaving is completed.

You can use the same tools and technique with *some* fabric strips — silks and silkies, lightweight T-shirt knits, anything not too heavy or bulky. Once you've woven your bands (zigzag stitch, tie or fringe the end to secure), you can use them as they are for trims and edgings. You can also zigzag stitch bands together to make mats, runners, bags or baskets.

The weaving goes very fast, and it's a marvelously mindless thing to

FIG. 7–5

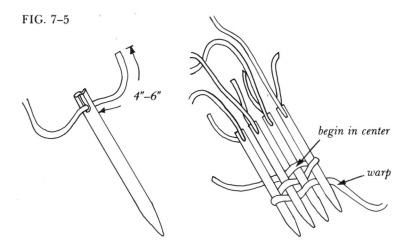

4"–6"

begin in center

warp

do while watching television or visiting. (And as a good friend of mine is fond of remarking, when they send you to the home, you'll be ready to go straight to the intermediate class.)

COILED BASKETS

You can make a coiled basket big enough for a baby's bassinet or a tiny cache-pot for a miniature house plant. The technique is the same — size depends on the diameter of your coiling base and the width of your strips. The technique is simple and fun. It's a good activity in which to involve your children on a rainy afternoon.

Let's go for a happy medium and pretend we're going to make a 10-inch-diameter round basket. Choose cord or rope about ½ inch in diameter and fabric strips around 1½ inches wide. Taper the end of the rope (see Fig. 7–6A), then wrap masking tape around the end (B). Thread the end of a fabric strip through a big needle and begin wrapping 4 inches from the tip as shown (C). Wrap the strip around the cord five or six times, then join to the next row by taking the strip around two coils (D). As you add coils, wrap loops of fabric over the preceding row to join and shape (E).

When the bottom is big enough, begin shaping up the sides by pulling a little tighter as you wrap. In this way, you'll be able to control

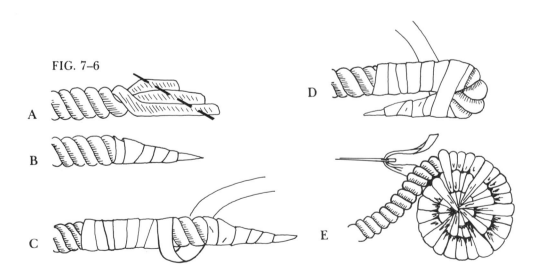

FIG. 7–6

A

B

C

D

E

FIG. 7–7

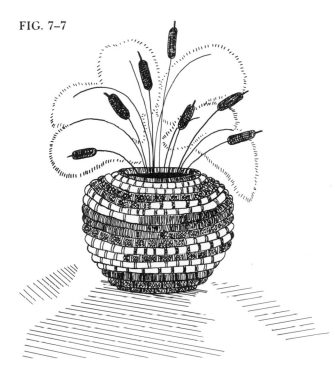

the shape, producing either a gentle or sharp curve. To add a new length of fabric strip, just overlap ends an inch or so; it's faster and easier than tying knots or taking a stitch.

To finish the basket, taper the end of the cord and wrap it neatly to the top of the basket, then run the end of the strip under two or three previous wraps to secure.

FLOP BOXES

Flop boxes are neat, storage-efficient little containers. They store flat when you don't need them, then four knots later you have a box—for presenting cookies, storing lingerie, or whatever. If you make them with the log cabin quilt method or another strip-piecing method, you can use some of your strips. Even making them of whole cloth requires very little fabric, depending of course on the size box you want.

You've probably seen these already in fancy shops, especially around Christmas. Although the concept is clever in general, for holi-

FIG. 7–8 *In the cardboard-stiffened flop box shown here, ribbons are tied to form a box shape. Note how the corners, left unstiffened, fold to the inside, forming little pockets. The box was designed by Claire Shaeffer, who chose a seasonal print and a coordinating pindot.*

FIG. 7–9 *Loretta Daum Byrne's Easter basket is made by the flop-box technique, omitting cardboard. Sides and ends fold up and tie together with ribbons. Loretta used log-cabin piecing to form the ends, strip-piecing for the sides, and added crocheted doilies and buttons.*

day decor it's downright brilliant. Who among us has space for storing Easter baskets, Halloween centerpieces or Valentine candy gift boxes? Flop boxes made up in seasonal prints and combinations, though, stack flat in any old box or suitcase.

You can insert lightweight cardboard into the sewn pockets of the box to stabilize it, or strip-piece over heavy batting. The cardboard method, of course, will give you a harder, crisper look. Made without cardboard, though, the flop box is washable. Here are basics for both styles of box.

Cut two squares of fabric; let's say 8 inches each. Pin ribbon or fabric loop ties to one square as shown in Figure 7–10; layer the second fabric square on top, right sides facing. Stitch ¼ inch or so from the edge, leaving an opening along one side between ties. Clip corners, turn and press.

Cut cardboard sections to fit the box. You'll need four rectangles to form the sides, a larger square for the bottom. The squares at the corners are left as they are to enable the box to fold when tied. Slip the cardboard pieces in between the layers of fabric through the opening you've left. Hold them in place and stitch as shown in Figure 7–11. Slip stitch or machine topstitch the opening closed; tie ribbons to form box.

For a softer box, layer outer fabric and lining (right sides facing), then batting on top. Pin ties in place. Stitch through all layers, leaving

FIG. 7–10

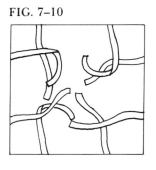

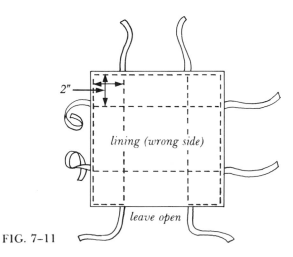

FIG. 7–11

FIG. 7–12

one edge open. (This style box uses no cardboard.) Follow these directions to make box sides and ends of any size you like. Trim away excess batting from the seam allowances and turn to the right side. Machine quilt to hold the layers in place.

For the box bottom, sandwich batting between outer fabric and lining, then machine quilt, leaving ½ inch or so around the edges unquilted.

Sew sides and ends to bottom, right sides facing, and stitching only the outer fabric and batting. Leave the lining fabric free. Trim away excess batting and slip stitch lining fabric over seam. Attach ties now if you chose not to incorporate them into the sewing together of the layers.

Though these directions are general, all sections of both styles of boxes can be strip-pieced, crazy quilted or pieced almost any way you'd like. Flop boxes are a super way to use up seasonal prints.

BRAIDED WREATHS

Although there are ways to braid any number of strands or tubes, we're most familiar with the common pigtail or three-strand braid. Decide on

FIG. 7–13 *This kitchen wreath by Cicely Hursh is composed of three stuffed braids; a total of nine strips in all. Cicely goes on to add a padded bow and hand-painted kitchen utensils.*

the finished size (circumference) of the circle you want to make, then cut nine strips that long, adding a little extra for seams and stuffing take-up—from 2 to 6 inches wide. To stuff each tube, you'll need fat cotton cording, strips of bonded batting, or whatever you can thread through the tubes to fill them. Say your strips are 3 inches wide. Seam the long sides together, right sides facing, in a narrow seam. Turn to the right side and stuff the tubes.

Braid in groups of three, then braid those groups together. Hand stitch the ends together, flattening and perfecting the circle as you stitch. Sew on a hanging loop, and you're done. Of course you can go on to add all sorts of embellishments if you like—bows, ribbons, Christmas ornaments, stuffed shapes.

Cicely Hursh, of San Carlos, California, shares another method for fabric wreaths. Cut a length of heavy coathanger wire the length (circumference) of your desired circle, plus enough extra to bend into loops on either end as shown in Figure 7–14.

After stitching and turning one fabric strip, insert the wire. Hook the ends together and slip stitch the ends of the fabric strip to close it and completely hide the wire. With this strong base, stuffed fabric tubes can be looped and wound around, with a few stitches here and there

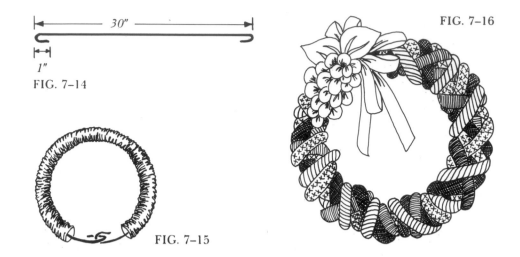

FIG. 7–14

FIG. 7–15

FIG. 7–16

anchoring them to the fabric-covered wire. Of course you can use braided tubes, too.

OUTDOOR STUFF (A DISCOURAGING WORD)

I've seen directions for strip-pieced lawn chair covers, patio cushions and wind socks. Don't do it! Oh, you can sew on a stripe or two, a watermelon or sailboat appliqué. But keep physics in mind, your form and function. Any item which must withstand heavy wear and outdoor conditions should be as simple and whole-cloth as possible. Within sight as I write are two formerly gorgeous whipped-by-Texas-winds windsocks. Handmade, lovingly stitched pieces that each lasted about a month. Also in sight is a stunning polished cotton multi-colored strip-pieced lawn chair cover. It's embarrassing to ask your friend whether their weight exceeds 120 pounds before offering them a chair. The lesson: Save your time, your energy, your blossoming expertise for wearables, indoor decor, and gifts.

Once I read a book that showed how to make a variety of furniture items from pieced leather. The authors recommended using suede splits—the weak, fibrous layer underneath the smooth leather exterior. Now even a leather split jacket is going to have a brief and tenuous life, and it broke my heart to think of these poor, misguided people buying their leather, piecing it (no easy task) and watching it rip at the seams, rip down the middle. And we won't even talk about the strip-pieced terry cloth seat covers I once made for my VW van. . .

EMBROIDERING WITH FABRIC

There's a beautiful and unusual book in print called *Making Needlecraft Landscapes*, by Mary Carroll (see Suggested Reading). (One of the unusual aspects of the book is that it's a fund-raising effort co-sponsored by the British Needlecrafts Council and the Women's National Cancer Control Campaign.) While admiring the fine works pictured, I came across what looked like a hand-woven tapestry. Intrigued, I looked more closely — not woven, but embroidered with ¼-inch strips of lightweight fabrics on loosely woven backing. The designer, Christine Sayers, used strips of voile, chiffon and lining fabrics threaded through a large-eyed needle to work straight stitches about ⅜ inch long, using no different methods than had she been working with floss or yarn. The finished picture, a lake with mountain peaks in the background, shimmers and beckons. In my experiments with the technique, I left the ends unsecured on the wrong side of the embroidery, figuring that the tension of the fabric threads around them would hold them in place and that if used as a picture, there'd be no reason for the strips ever to pull out. I also found that pre-washed fabric strips are immeasurably easier to work with.

bits

Other than the discussion in Chapter 1, not much needs to be said about trimming and storing those fabric scraps that fit into the "bits" category. Those state-of-the-art strippers and cutters we talked about earlier won't be of any help here. It's going to be pretty much you, your rotary cutter and your scissors.

The important thing in dealing with bits is to keep your options open. Unless you want to grab a template and have a perfect 4-inch square at the ready, the best thing to do with scrap bits is to trim the tags and put the bits into a clear plastic box or bag. It's true that the boxes take up more room than hanging bags, but the advantage is that far less pressing of the scraps is needed when you begin to work with them. I stack these boxes and folded yardage on utility steel shelving.

QUILTS

As we talk about six methods of making scrap quilts, we'll omit almost all mention of technique. You can find this general information anywhere. Go to the library. The more you prowl the aisles for books on art, needlecraft, costume and surface design, the more the librarians will recognize your need and interest. Your avid search could trigger the purchase of more reference books.

A recommended article: "Out of Control: Quilts that Break the Rules" by Barbara Brackman in *The Quilt Digest*, 1985. A bizarre collection of seven startling quilts gives us a good whack on the side of the head as to what a quilt should be. Everything *The Quilt Digest* and attendant subsidiaries have published so far has been stellar.

TRIP AROUND THE WORLD

One of the oldest and simplest of quilt patterns, Trip Around the World lends itself perfectly to scrap quilts. My first three or four quilts were made in this pattern. To begin with, you can take your favorite squares and place them right in the center for impact; they become the center medallion.

You'll have more fun with your quilt if you lay out every single square before you begin sewing. It's really gratifying to move one corner square here and come up with something clever and balancing there. And once you have the quilt laid out, stacking and sewing the squares is marvelously mindless.

FIG. 8–1 *Although Judy Florence's nautical wall hanging doesn't look like a scrap quilt at first glance, the sailboats could certainly be made of scraps you have on hand. Judy chose polka-dots on white background fabric to make the sails bright and festive.*

Start in the center of your layout space and place your favorite pieces in the center, forming a diamond shape as shown in Figure 8–3. Fill in all the area with squares. Create diagonal stripes in the corners, matching or teasing the eye. After your desired design area is filled in, stack up the squares beginning with the lefthand vertical row. Pick them up from the lower edge of the quilt so that when you have them all in your hand they're in order with the bottom square on top. Sew it to the second square, the second to the third, etc., to make a long strip. Lay that strip on your layout board and get the pieces for the second strip. Sew it in the same way, continuing across the quilt until all the vertical strips are assembled.

Press all seams to one side. If a dark square adjoins a light one,

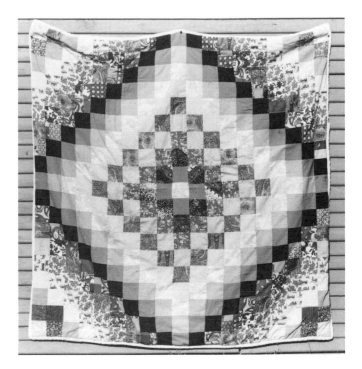

FIG. 8–2 *This ancient and well-loved "Trip Around the World" quilt is one of two that I made for my twin daughters when they were three years old. The girls are nineteen now, taking their quilts and leaving home. Although the quilts need new binding, that's the only sign of the hard wear and machine washing they've been through. Photograph by the author.*

press toward the dark color. If one fabric has noticeably more body than an adjacent piece, press toward the limper, more giving fabric. Pin the first strip to the second, pinning at seams for accurate matching. Pin and sew all strips to complete the quilt top.

Cheating: If strips are not perfectly equal, pin at corners for visual

FIG. 8–3

matching. Pleat, gather or stretch in between the corners to fit. This is a scrap quilt. Do you really want to rip out those seams and re-sew them? As you continue the process, you'll automatically get better. Press all the long seams to one side, then tack up on a wall and admire! These quilts can be real eye-dazzlers.

Lately, quilt artists have stretched Trip Around the World into rectangles for a different look.

CRAZY QUILTS (OR, HYACINTHS TO FEED THY SOUL)

Crazy quilts are the traditional showcase for precious tiny bits of silk, velvet and satin, used pretty much "as is" and heavily encrusted with embroidery. Often scorned by serious critics, these admittedly outrageous creations fascinate most of us. As Mae West said, "Too much of a good thing is delightful."

I've tried and tried to accomplish crazy piecing on the sewing machine and have never been happy with the results. Mary Conroy, author of *The Complete Book of Crazy Patchwork*, casts my problems only a glancing nod. To begin with, you just plain can't sew the necessary seams on the sewing machine. Mary says to sew what you can on the machine, then do the impossible ones by hand. She also addresses my second complaint that gaps remain between the patches on machine-sewn crazy quilts. "No problem there," she says, "machine appliqué a patch over it." Mary is a much more generous lady all around than I am. She even includes, in her excellent book on crazy patchwork, a method for making crazy quilts from polyester knit.

I do love Mary's idea for totally machine sewn crazy quilts. Rather than being overlapped, each piece is cut exactly to size, then the whole pattern is machine satin stitched in place. Either use black thread or thread leftovers in the process.

In the traditional method, of course, each piece on the block is pinned in place, then each seam turned under and slip stitched down, then a rich pastiche of embroidery stitches laid over each seam. All the marbles roll to the side of form in the crazy quilt. Not much function here. Don't wash it, don't use it roughly, or better yet, don't use it at all.

FIG. 8–4 *Crazy quilting doesn't have to produce a quilt. Designer and author Judith Montaño works extensively in crazy quilting, using it for clothing accents and jewelry. Here, one of her pillows illustrates a small project you can make to experiment with this delightful technique. (Check Suggested Reading for Judith's book on the subject.)*

Just look at it. That's all right, isn't it? Remember the ancient Persian proverb:

> If of thy mortal goods thou art bereft
> And of thy slender store, two loaves alone to thee are left,
> Sell one, and with the dole,
> Buy hyacinths to feed thy soul.

BISCUIT QUILTS

Old-fashioned biscuit quilts are simple, cozy quilts that lend themselves to take-along sewing bags, are equally suited to speedy machine sewing, and allow for a lot of creative design.

The building block, the "biscuit," is formed by sewing two mismatched squares or hexagons together. The top piece is larger than the bottom one; to align them, pleat the top piece along the seams and tuck in a ball of polyester fiberfill.

Because squares are easier, let's talk about them. If you really like biscuit quilts, you can figure out hexagons on your own or with the help of a book. To practice, cut backing squares from trash fabric, say 4 inch-

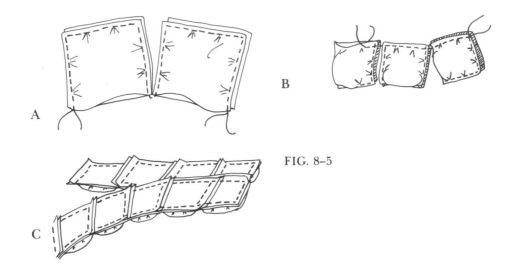

FIG. 8–5

es per side. Cut 5-inch quilt squares. Sew the top square to the bottom square, wrong sides facing and corners matching. To make them come out even, pleat the quilt square (the top square) once or twice per side (Fig. 8–5A). Sew a narrow seam — ⅛ or ¼ inch or so. Doris Carmack, author of *Easy Biscuit Quilting*, advises sewing assembly-line style. Sew around three sides, then sew right on to the next square. After you've sewn an entire strip together (B), stuff each biscuit, then machine stitch the open side together, again pleating where needed (C). Repeat for the second row, then sew rows together. Line the quilt, then tack or tie to lining. Bind if you like.

YOYO QUILTS

Yoyos have assumed their rightful place as kitsch supreme. For that reason, and because they are, after all, circles, which are always hard to come by, their inclusion is merited here. Someday, for who knows what perhaps inspired reason, you may want to include some in your work. So you ought to know how.

Cut circles no larger than 4 inches in diameter, run a gathering thread around ¼ inch from the edge, then draw up the thread to gather into a smaller circle. Tack the adjoining areas of the gathered circles together, and there you have it.

FIG. 8–6 *Alyssa Hofmann of Dallas, Texas, made this yoyo pillow in sherbet shades and surrounded it with a soft ruffle. It's a good example of a small project that lets you play with techniques without getting too involved.*

Although yoyos are discussed here under the heading of quilts, keep your mind open. I recently met a woman who creates ornate long dresses, gloves and headpieces from hundreds (thousands?) of yoyo circles. The bodice, of course, as well as other selected areas, is lined. Such a striking and unusual ensemble *does* attract attention.

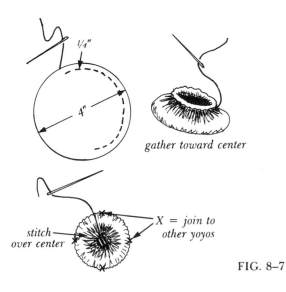

1/4"

4"

gather toward center

stitch over center

X = join to other yoyos

FIG. 8–7

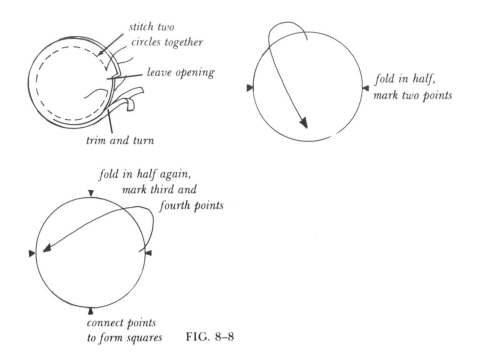

stitch two
circles together

leave opening

trim and turn

fold in half,
mark two points

fold in half again,
mark third and
fourth points

connect points
to form squares   FIG. 8–8

CIRCULAR PATCHWORK

Lois Bateman of McKenzie, Tennessee, came up with this clever technique, and it's shared here with her permission. The finished effect is vaguely similar to cathedral window quilting, but it's all done on the sewing machine. The only template or pattern you'll need is a plate or other circle.

Because both sides of each circle are visible in the finished, completely reversible quilt, the planning of color and pattern becomes an art in itself. The basic technique, however, is simple as pie. Sew two circles together, right sides facing, leaving a turn-opening. Turn to the right side.

After you've made enough circles (a 10-inch circle produces a 7-inch square; a circle 7 inches in diameter gives you a square about 5 inches per side), you can begin stitching them together to form squares. Fold them in half twice and mark four "corner" points as shown in Figure 8–8. The arcs left over (which will later be topstitched down) can wind up on either side of the quilt. For your first one, make it easy on yourself and stitch them to one side only.

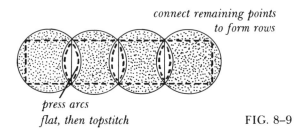

*connect remaining points
to form rows*

*press arcs
flat, then topstitch*   FIG. 8–9

Sew the circles together in rows as shown in Figure 8–9, then sew the rows together. Press the arcs open and topstitch. Even on the side where the arcs don't appear, you'll have topstitching lines showing to add interest to the design.

You can either leave the edges rounded when you finish or fold those arcs back and topstitch for a straight edge.

CHARM QUILTS

Aaaah, but charm quilts are a magical concept! Back in the late 1800s, charm quilts and charm strings were the latest thing. They both made a resurgence during the Depression when people found themselves with plenty of time and no money. A charm string was a love tool, a collection of 999 different buttons all strung together on a thread. When she added the 999th button to the string, a young girl believed she would soon see her true love appear.

In the same genre were charm quilts. Now here was a project to foster cooperation! Using only one template, make a quilt in which no fabric is ever repeated. Jinny Beyer has been working to recognize this art form; she's put together a respectable collection of charm quilts and has written about them extensively in her praiseworthy book, *The Scrap Look*. The tumbler was a popular motif, as were squares, rectangles and hexagons.

The most traditional form of charm quilt contained 999 pieces of fabric, all different, but beautiful examples exist with far fewer pieces, some with even more. It was enough of a challenge, I would think, to go about gathering up 999 different scraps of fabric that could be manipulated into an eye-pleasing arrangement, but that wasn't enough. The best charm quilts contain *trompe l'oeil* tricks — they fool the eye by clever juxtapositions of fabric *almost* identical.

There's obviously a lot more going on with a charm quilt than just covering up on a cold night. A myth surrounds the quilts: On the first night you sleep under a particular quilt, whatever you dream will come true.

The only word we need to say about technique is begin collecting now! (And read Chapter 13.)

APPLIQUE

A NEW WAY TO HAND APPLIQUE

Appliqué scares a lot of people, I think. It scared me until I learned an easy, neat way to produce perfect appliqué shapes. Geri Waechter of Omaha, Arkansas, taught me this technique, and it is used here with her permission.

Trace the appliqué pattern onto a piece of non-fusible interfacing, muslin, batiste or other "neutral" backing fabric (Fig. 9–1A). Lay the traced outline on the right side of your chosen appliqué fabric and sew all the way around on the sewing machine. Overlap the stitches at the beginning and end just a little. Now slash the backing fabric (B), turn the motif to the right side (C), and press carefully so that none of the backing shows on the front. Depending on the fabric weights you're working with, you might want to trim away most of the backing. Now use the standard tiny invisible stitches typical of classic hand appliqué to attach the motif to the background.

MACHINE APPLIQUE

It's impossible to praise machine appliqué too highly. It's time-efficient, easy to do, is usually sturdy and long-wearing, and can be exquisitely attractive. (This last attribute does require a certain skill.) Choose fabrics that are closely woven and fairly stable. Kettle Cloth, Indian Head, and good broadcloths are good to start with. After you've got the knack,

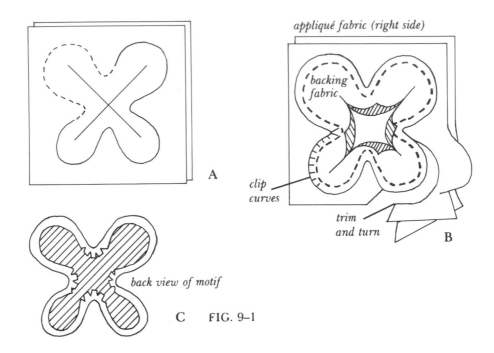

appliqué fabric (right side)

backing fabric

clip curves

trim and turn

A

B

back view of motif

C   FIG. 9–1

you can work with trickier fabrics. Keep shapes simple at first, too. Practice on the elm leaf, *then* go on to the full-plumage bird of paradise.

Adhesives and fusibles make today's machine appliqué practically fool-proof. You can choose between fabric glue sticks (Clotilde says the formula for all glue sticks is the same and that you can save money by buying the school-supply type rather than those marketed specially to stitchers), fabric glues, fusible webbing. All will hold your appliqué mo-

FIG. 9–2 *For a fast and easy baby gift, designer Chris Pfefferkorn of Plano, Texas, machine appliqués heart-shaped balloons cut from bright colors of fabric onto white piqué bibs. Chris adds highlights with a curved line of machine satin stitch, tapering at the ends.*

FIG. 9–3 Machine appliqué can be as elegant as you like; just vary fabric selection and design. Marsha Eckstrom made this dressy vest from black velveteen, then used a combination of machine appliqué and machine embroidery to work the peacock on the back. Bird's body is white satin; leaves are moiré taffeta, and tail feathers are a combination of satin, taffeta, velvet and velour.

tif securely in place while you stitch it on. Pins and basting still work, too.

Set your machine for a zigzag stitch, deciding width depending on the appliqué fabric. You need a fairly wide stitch to produce a strong appliqué. Shorten the stitch length until the stitches lie side by side neatly without piling up. You should loosen your top tension just a little so that no bobbin thread shows on the top. Ideally, the swing of the needle should just clear the appliqué shape. It's easy to follow the outline of the motif around, keeping the needle right on the line. Slow down around curves; stop and pivot at sharp curves and corners. You can, if you want an absolutely perfect stitch, pull threads to the back and tie them. If that's not so important, just stitch past where you began to lock threads.

Machine appliqué uses a lot of thread. If you collect thread like you collect fabric, of course, you can use this to your advantage. Appliqué thread does not have to match the appliqué fabric; in fact, richer textures can be achieved using slight variations, shadings and high contrast.

(For all you'll ever need to know about machine appliqué, see Robbie and Tony Fanning's comprehensive *The Complete Book of Machine Embroidery*. It's listed in Suggested Reading, along with *Pizzazz for Pennies*, by Barb Forman, focusing on machine appliqué for children.)

TRANSPARENCY IN APPLIQUE

There really isn't a lot you can do with scraps of organdy, organza, gauze, voile and netting. After you've made pot scrubbers out of your nylon net, that still leaves you with your stash of sheer fabrics. What you *can* do with sheer fabrics is build up layers of shading and texture by appliquéing them to another surface.

If you don't think you're an artist, one of the easiest jumping-off places for free design is a landscape. By the time you imagine your horizon, your mountain ranges or rolling hills, towering pines and clouds, you've got your basic design all done. This works with any fabrics (or paint or paper), and when you're using sheers, the landscapes become fog-shrouded Oriental mysteries.

In addition to clothing and art pieces, consider using transparent appliqué for curtains. Light diffuses beautifully passing through the subtle filters of fabric. Use basic machine appliqué techniques for applying the layers unless you're working on a serious piece, where hand appliqué adds to the delicacy possible with sheer layers.

One of the most beautiful examples I've seen of transparency for window coverings appears in *Decorative Home Sewing*, Ballantine Books (see Suggested Reading) and is described here with Ballantine's permission. Although it's shown as a no-sew technique, I'd amend it somewhat. Triangles of different colors of nylon net are affixed with metal eyelets to a plain white net curtain. The triangles are not aligned. Sets of two or three triangles, overlapping at random, are scattered freely over the base curtain. (I'd machine appliqué them in place with a widely spaced zigzag stitch to prevent the net triangles from drooping.) You can imagine what a beautiful play of light would result from this technique, especially as the light weight of the net would allow the slightest breeze to stir the curtain.

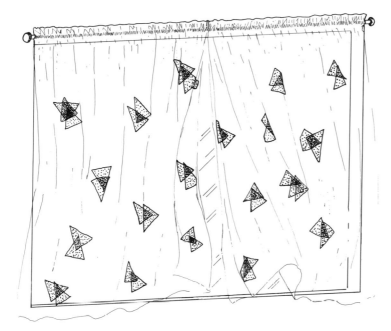

FIG. 9–4

REVERSE APPLIQUE

The most well-known examples of reverse appliqué are molas, the folk art of Panama's Cuna Indians. Their colorful blocks of geometrical or animal motifs are traditionally used as shirt and jacket yokes and have now achieved status with art collectors. Charlotte Patera's excellent books on the subject, *Cutwork Applique* and *Mola Making*, are listed in Suggested Reading. (From Charlotte, too, comes this note: Molas are *not* totally reverse appliqué. Exploding this myth seems to be impossible, but many elements in molas are appliquéd on top. And no more than four layers are ever used.) The photographs of traditional molas in this section were generously shared from Charlotte's remarkable collection.

To work the traditional method of reverse appliqué, baste together several layers of fabric, all the same size. Then cut through different layers to expose the colors beneath. Turn edges under just slightly, then secure with tiny hand stitches.

Because most molas are fairly small (from 10 to 24 inches, square

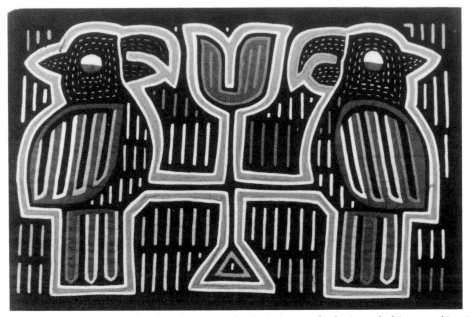

FIG. 9–5 *This multi-colored traditional mola, depicting two birds, is worked in a combination of reverse and traditional appliqué. The strips forming the birds' wings, tails and eyes, as well as the tulip-like flower blossom at top center, are all appliquéd on top. Photograph by Charlotte Patera.*

or rectangular, are common sizes), you can make them from scrap quantities of cotton fabrics. It's possible, too, to cheat, or shall we say improvise, by adding small pieces of fabric placed strategically underneath larger layers. Baste loosely to hold in place, then cut away the top layer in the shape desired.

It's important in reverse appliqué to cut only a short distance ahead of the securing stitches. Cut a few inches, turn under the edges and stitch, then cut a few more.

If the multi-layered effect of reverse appliqué appeals to you, but you're put off by the thought of all that careful hand stitching, consider the machine method. Stack several layers of fabric together, baste around the edges, then work closely spaced machine satin stitch in closed designs—circles, hearts or diamonds, for instance. Cut through selected layers next to the stitches. Just as with traditional reverse appliqué, you can add smaller pieces of fabric where you want them.

FIG. 9–6 *This fantastic creature (an alligator?) is typical of traditional mola designs. Photograph by Charlotte Patera.*

FIG. 9–7 *Here's a close-up detail of the diamond-shaped designs on the alligator. These diamonds are appliquéd on top. Photograph by Charlotte Patera.*

FIG. 9–8 *Reverse appliqué isn't a quick technique, but it's easy and allows wide scope in designing. This free-form design, "And Waves," by Diane Kernell, originally took shape as a small coverlet or wall hanging. It would work as a table runner, mat or clothing element. Cutting through only one layer of fabric, as Diane did, is a simplified version of the multi-layered cut-turn-and-stitch method used by the Cuna Indians of Panama in their colorful molas.*

FIG. 9–9 *Just imagine turning under all the edges of this intricate snowflake pattern to hand appliqué it! Machine appliqué wouldn't be any easier. Using the technique of shadow appliqué, though, designer Lois Winston of Elkins Park, Pennsylvania, makes it simple to produce, and the softening effect of the sheer white fabric overlay is especially fine on a snowflake.*

Shadow appliqué, quilting, and trapunto rely on the visual effects of see-through fabrics, too, but are used in conjunction with brightly colored accent fabrics and yarns. This is a good way to use up other fabric scraps, too.

Shadow appliqué begins with a backing piece of muslin, old sheet, or some similar lightweight white or off-white fabric the approximate size of the finished piece. Lightly draw in the major design areas right on the backing fabric. Lay appliqué pieces in place and hold with a bit of glue or webbing. Over this, lay the sheer fabric. You'll see at once that the colors are muted, softened and blended together, opening up new possibilities for color combination.

Hand stitch around each appliqué shape through all layers. Use white, pastel or even bright-colored thread for different effects. Once you begin stitching, you'll see the second eye-opening characteristic of this technique — you can cut the most complicated shapes you want, because there are no edges to be turned under, no tricky pivot-points to negotiate.

If you're a determined machine stitcher, though, it's possible to sew around simple shapes on the machine. If more intricate shapes beckon you, consider working the stitch with free-motion technique.

FIG. 9–10 *To embellish the lid of her hexagonal fabric box, Charlyne Stewart of Los Angeles, California, places two gingko leaves cut from felt. The sheer overlay makes a delicate Oriental design even more effective. Charlyne adds hand embroidery details to each leaf.*

Loosen the top tension, remove the presser foot and lower the feed dogs of your machine. Put the basted fabric layers in a hoop and stitch away. Check your sewing machine manual for details on how to set up your machine for free-motion embroidery, or look at any of the good books available on the subject (see Suggested Reading).

STRAIGHT-STITCH APPLIQUE

This is almost too easy. When I first saw a sample of Jackie Dodson's straight-stitch appliqué method, I could hardly wait to try it. Even better than shadow work for enabling you to use tricky shapes (and maintain intense colors), this technique is rich in possibilities. The piece I saw featured appliquéd circles. Jackie had used coins for templates to cut circles from bright, solid-color cottons. She arranged them at random on a backing fabric, overlapping some to form concentric circles.

After fusing the circles in place with fusible webbing (you could use glue stick or your favorite fusing method), Jackie used a fade-away or

FIG. 9–11 *Use the fusible webbing method to attach circles to the background fabric, then stitch evenly spaced lines of straight stitching to hold them there.*

wash-out marker to mark parallel lines ½ inch apart all over the design. She straight stitched along the marked lines, then used them for a guide to fill in more parallel straight lines until lines covered the surface of the stitchery ⅛ inch apart. This multitude of stitches holds the appliqué motifs quite firmly in place and imparts a rich texture.

Jackie Dodson's fine book, *Know Your Bernina*, (see Suggested Reading) contains more material on this technique, as well as many more of interest even to non-Bernina owners.

CLOTHING

HIDDEN SIDE-SEAM POCKETS

There's nothing radical about the concept of using a different fabric for side-seam pockets, patch pocket linings or welt pocket linings. Usually the added bulk of making these with the self-fabric would be unattractive and difficult to manipulate.

Instead of buying the ¼ yard listed on the pattern envelope, though, consider using what you have on hand. All those lining-weight fabrics can be used, as well as broadcloth, silk, muslin, or whatever weight and drape works well with your fashion fabric. Why not have polka-dot or houndstooth-check pocket linings? It's more fun.

Consider putting pockets into the side seams of your dresses, jackets and skirts even if the pattern doesn't call for them. There's nothing easier. Cut four pockets similar to the diagram in Figure 10–1—they needn't be exact. Make sure you have 6 or 7 inches for hand insertion.

Pin pockets where you want them along front and back side seams; stitch as pinned. Press seams toward pocket. Sew side seam to pocket, double stitch for reinforcement, then pivot and stitch around pocket curve. Reinforce at corner again, pivot, and finish sewing the side seam. Clip the back seam allowance at top and bottom of pocket. Press the seam open, the pocket forward. Pink, zigzag or otherwise finish the seams.

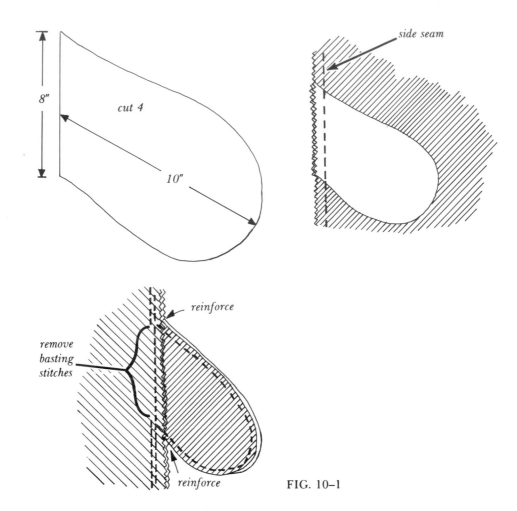

FIG. 10–1

FACINGS

Almost everything we said about side-seam pockets can also be said about facings. It's no longer *de rigueur* to have self-fabric or even matching facings. You can tastefully match print with print, color with color. So go for it. Not only will combining fabrics give you wider options on the accumulation you already have, it will save you money in the future. Why hide $12 a yard, 14-inch-wide Japanese cotton in facings that only the laundry will see? (Yes, Japanese cotton must be ironed.) When the difference might mean $40, why insist on self-facings? You should be choosy and careful about combining fabrics of varied fiber content. My considerations are mainly esthetic, but no doubt physical properties do enter into it.

A freedom with facings can lead you into some fearless designing, too. Don't like the collar? Ditch it! Simple, uncluttered necklines lend themselves more readily to jewelry and frame a face better, too. Don't like the sleeves? Don't have enough fabric for the sleeves? Face the armholes. Face the whole situation.

Here are two ways to make facings for patterns that weren't designed for them. First, the proper way: Lay a piece of tissue over the garment pattern you'll be facing. Let's say it's the bodice front. Trace right over the neckline, the shoulderline and the front opening, if there is one. Measure several points two or three inches out from the neckline. The facing width depends on fabric weight, fabric supply, pattern style, and your personal preference. Use a French curve to connect the points. There's your facing pattern. You can improve on it if you have sufficient fabric by laying the adjacent pattern piece alongside the first—in this case it would be the bodice back. Pin or tape that pattern piece to eliminate a seam. Cut the entire facing in one piece to reduce bulk and save time. If there's not enough fabric, don't let that stand between you and what you want. Piece, trim and press.

Next, the laissez-faire method: Mark the desired width of the facing along the shoulderline. Trace neckline, shoulderline and front opening. Remove pattern and cut the facing free-hand.

Nancy Zieman's version of this method is ingenious. She recommends waxed paper and your trusty 6-inch hem gauge. Place the waxed paper over the pattern, then mark neckline and shoulderline on the waxed paper. Then turn the hem gauge on its side, set the pointer for desired depth of facing, and run the gauge over the desired facing cutting line. The pointer will mark the waxed paper, and your facing pattern's ready to cut out.

FABRIC JEWELRY

Get out your prettiest, most treasured bits. Look at books with color photographs of jewelry by Lalique and other masters of the art. Cut out some cardboard templates of your favorite shapes. Try circles, trian-

FIG. 10–2 *These pendant necklaces are made from small bits of floral print fabrics. Designer Carol Pladsen of Caldwell, Idaho, couches gold thread around selected motifs, adds embroidery stitches, and mounts the circle of fabric on cardboard. Backed with fabric and wrapped 'round with satin cord, they're ready to wear.*

gles, moons, fans and hearts. Cut two matching shapes, embellish one with beads, appliqué or embroidery, then machine stitch it to its facing shape. Stuff lightly and slip stitch the opening closed. Make a thread or thin fabric loop; affix to tube necklace, silk cording or even a metal chain.

Judith Montaño's crazy quilt pendants are a fine example of what can be done with fabric jewelry. Judith uses crazy quilting, punchneedle embroidery and beads to embellish a heart shape, then

FIG. 10–3

pads it lightly, backs it with leather and sews cording around the edges. I have one of these that Judith made, and it never fails to attract attention. Judith, from Castle Rock, Colorado, also works with fan shapes to produce similar pendants.

SCARVES AND TIES

After completing the S for the cover of this book, I had plenty of small bits of silk left over. Most were about 3 inches long, some shorter, and of varied widths. "Why," I asked myself, "can't I strip piece these together and make a little scarf?"

I cut a piece of batiste 3 by 25 inches, drew curves at either end with an air-erasable marker, and began piecing. It took only about 30 minutes to cover the backing.

Since I had colors in the red-pink range and in the blue-green range, my love of hand laundry took over. If colors bled slightly into their neighbors on the color wheel, no harm would be done. I divided the scraps into these two groups for that reason. After pressing the patchwork, I machine stitched it to a silk backing, turned it to the right side and slip stitched the turn opening closed. It's a marvelous accessory, almost free in the realms of time *and* money.

The same method could be used for an obi belt, narrow wrap-and-tie sash or choker.

COLLAGED VESTS AND JACKETS

You can use "bits" to collage clothing in a myriad of ways, from checkerboard squares to free-form crazy quilting. If, however, you've ever seen a jacket pieced from double-knit polyester in catch-as-catch-can fashion, you will realize that reticence must prevail. *Everything* just doesn't look good together, except in nature. God mixes colors and textures with a mastery we only glimpse. So limit your palette. Try blues or ivory/creams.

Keep fabric weights in mind as well as colors. All those seams will contribute bulk. While a pieced denim fabric may be ideal for a quilt, window warmer or rug, it might not be comfortable as a wearable.

See the color section for Barbara State's exquisite pieced jumper bib, made of tiny bits of wool and cashmere, and Betsy Hatch's beautiful landscape vest. Both these examples of collaged clothing prove that these garments can be tasteful and professional. They're a far cry from the double-knit polyester.

Try collaging just a portion of a garment. A yoke, collar, cuffs, or an arbitrarily color-blocked area can often make a far stronger statement than would the over-all embellished surface.

Remember that if you collage a part of a garment, you will be drawing the eye of the viewer to that part. Use this knowledge wisely. If you are a petite person, do not embellish at the hemline only. A good rule of thumb in clothing design in general, and collaged clothing in particular, is that the garment should not overshadow the wearer. No matter how tall, short, thin or fluffy you may be, embellishment around the face is always flattering. If you pride yourself on beautiful hands, focus on cuffs and sleeve tips. If your shoulders are the stuff men's dreams are made of, flaunt them with collaged camisoles, sundresses with bands of trim at the top. Tiny waist? Well, you get the picture.

COLLAGED SKIRTS AND PANTS

My first thought was that this section could be the shortest, most concise one in the book. It could consist of a single word: Don't.

Ah, those blanket condemnations, how they sneak up on our blind sides! True, I have never seen a pieced skirt or trousers I would wear outside my backyard, but then that's *overall* piecing. Think about bands of trim around a hemline, collaged pockets, even a vertical strip to draw the eye in a lengthy sweep up the leg; these would be workable, wearable ways to embellish the "nether garments."

It's still a short section. But instead of "don't," it's "just watch it— that's all."

PRAIRIE POINTS

Placing prairie points in the clothing section is highly arbitrary. After all, we've seen these little geometric figures in and around quilts, too,

FIG. 10–4 *Simple checkerboard squares embellish parts of these vests for mother and daughter. Designer Marguerite Snow added buttons from her collection.*

and in Chapter 11 we'll talk about prairie point rugs. They're here with clothing for two main reasons. The first time I ever worked with prairie points was in Yvonne Porcella's silk painting workshop where we made strip pieced vests. I tucked a few here and there into the seams, then tacked them down with beads. That, too, is a personal and arbitrary reason. Prairie point buttonholes, now, that's a real reason. And we'll get to it later.

Prairie points are just squares folded into triangles in either of two ways, shown in Figure 10–5. As you see, you get a triangle that opens either on the side or in the middle. If you want to overlap the prairie

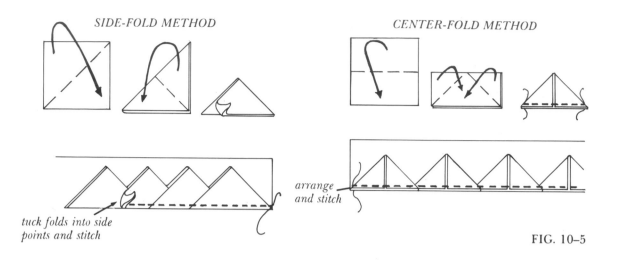

SIDE-FOLD METHOD

CENTER-FOLD METHOD

tuck folds into side points and stitch

arrange and stitch

FIG. 10–5

points, it's neat to tuck one inside the other, so make them with side openings. If the points will abut but not overlap, or if you want to use them for buttonholes (we're getting to it), you want a center opening.

If, during your sorting process, you elected to cut some squares ranging from 4 to 8 inches, you'll find these to be perfect for prairie points.

Have you ever worked long and hard to produce a decent, if not perfect, garment and then messed up a buttonhole? Now it's true that a prairie point buttonhole is not a closure you want to use on everything, but it's another handy trick to have up your sleeve. It's sporty, ethnic or western, depending on how you use it.

After you're through with your center-opening prairie point, just make your buttonhole in the very center between the folds. Add it to

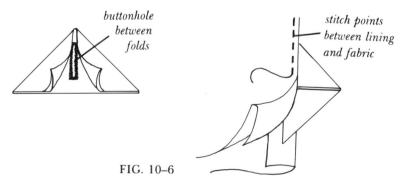

buttonhole between folds

stitch points between lining and fabric

FIG. 10–6

the garment as you would button loops, securing between front and facing or in the seam binding. It's the same old buttonhole technique, and you still might mess one up. But if you do, toss out that triangle and start again. Use your best five out of six.

LITTLE BUTTERFLIES

In Saks Fifth Avenue, I almost ran across the sales floor to see what turned out to be a $3,000 evening gown. From a distance it looked as if the sleeves were covered with butterflies. The closer I got, the more mysterious grew the metamorphosis. It turned out to be nothing more than twists of silk organza, all with unfinished raw edges, tacked down in the center with a stitch or two, as shown in Figure 10–7.

How would you clean or press this gown? Is that like asking the price of the yacht? If you have to ask, you can't afford it?

Because the stitches are almost entirely hidden by the full gathers of the butterfly, you could bar-tack them on the sewing machine. If you want your butterflies less stylized, here's how to do it: Trace around a simple half-butterfly shape onto doubled fabric, as shown in Figure 10–8. Unfold the fabric and lay it on another layer of the same fabric or a coordinating piece. Machine satin stitch all the way around, then trim close to the stitching. Pleat or gather a little along the center line if you like, then stitch to the base fabric with a line of machine satin stitching. Depending on how fancy you feel and how many of these little crea-

FIG. 10–7

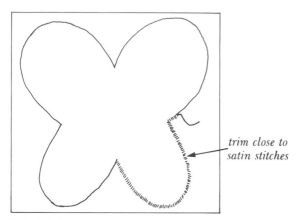

trim close to satin stitches

FIG. 10–8

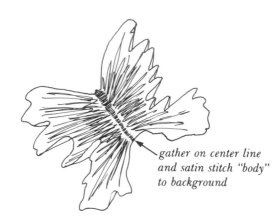

gather on center line and satin stitch "body" to background

FIG. 10–9 *Patti Felsen's little "Engineer Bear" is only twelve inches tall, wears a tiny vest and cap made from scraps of ticking-striped cotton.*

FIG. 10–10 *You can use up snippets of lace and other trims as well as scraps of fabric making doll clothes. Shown here, a dress, pinafore and bonnet made by Cheryl Robertson of Dallas, Texas. The doll is handcrafted by Joyce and Ken Ensey (see Sources of Supply).*

tures you're manufacturing, you may want to taper the satin stitch to more closely resemble a butterfly's body.

These would also be beautiful on curtains or a bedspread.

DOLL AND BABY CLOTHES

Almost any old doll, dressed with skill and imagination, has charm. All babies are beautiful, no matter whether they're dressed or not, but the baby should be comfortable. That's almost all one needs to say about the subject. Pattern prints, if used, should be small in scale. Fabrics should be supple, drapable.

Doll cloths are made either for an on-the-spot demand (Esmerelda's winter coat or a miniature replica of your black satin skirt), loving gifts, or to make money. With each new doll craze, the opportunity to sell clothing for that doll beckons.

And you can use your scrap fabrics for doll clothing. Remember a few basic truths. Unless you're making an heirloom-to-be, keep it simple and make it easy on yourself. Eliminate facings, seams, darts. Keep pattern pieces and details to a minimum. Let the fabric make a strong, stylish statement. A silver lamé sash or red Ultrasuede appliqué makes more sense on a doll dress than do handmade tucks. If you're interested in selling doll clothing, you'll have to make every step count in order to make a profit. Go for speed and style.

I see no reason why a baby shouldn't wear a black jacket with rose-pink blossoms printed on it, if the fabric is soft and has a high natural fiber content. Babies in exotic lands are often dressed in navy blue or bright red. Pink is no more comfortable. Stretch your horizons a little in dressing baby. (See Suggested Reading for an excellent book on the subject.)

HOUSEHOLD ITEMS

WALLAGE (RHYMES WITH COLLAGE)

Gail Brown, author of the fine series, *Instant Interiors*, as well as another of my favorite books about silk, taught me that liquid starch will adhere fabrics to walls, furniture and appliances. I always intended to cover my bathroom walls this way, and I checked with Gail to make sure the excessive humidity wouldn't be a problem. "No," she assured me, "go ahead. It'll work." But as time passed, I couldn't figure out a way to cope with the broken metal tiles on the lower part of the walls. I felt I could live with broken white tiles while I solved that problem, but life with poison yellow vinyl wallpaper soon wore thin. I really didn't want to waste fabric that might later be covered by tile, and I certainly didn't want to stop short of the future tile line with my fabric. What to do? Well, we all know what invention is born of, don't we?

"Why not," I reasoned, "use scraps? That way, it'll be easy to add more to match if the tile doesn't come up high enough to cover. And it'll cover up the ugly walls." I peeled off the vinyl, exposing an equally unattractive dark blue wallpaper.

Next I sorted through my small cotton and cotton-blend scraps, choosing primary colors, black and white. I trimmed them to approximate squares and rectangles, leaving a diagonal cut here and there and mixing pinked with straight-cut edges. Quantity needed was sheer guesswork.

I handed these scraps and a half-gallon of liquid starch to my teenaged daughter, Lacy. "Here," I said, "see what you can do with this." It wasn't what I would have done. It was looser, freer, well. . .it was better. The moral of this story is: Let your kids do it. I'll tell you what, though—I'm doing the next one. She liked it a lot.

It took Lacy two or three easy sessions to complete the bathroom walls. They've been up over a year, the tile is still in process, and except for a little ripple here and there (easy to fix—just re-apply starch and stick down), the wallage looks as good as when it was put up.

In our family room is a big, ugly pale green wallpapered wall. I plan to sort through and separate my ivory/cream/beige pieces and do a subtle, almost marbleized wall for that room. The technique is exceedingly simple: Brush liquid starch onto a clean, smooth surface. Dip each piece of fabric into a bowl of starch, apply to the wall and smooth out.

LAMP SHADES

There is something absolutely magical about light coming through color. Stained glass windows, of course, are the highest example of this phenomenon. (I once lived happily in an apartment that could charitably be called a dump, because it had seven stained glass windows, one on the west side being deep red.) With certain fabrics and certain windows, we can achieve a luminous effect with curtains, but the sad fact is that they fade. Lamp shades, however, are the perfect place to exploit the color and light combination. Many lamps are small enough that a whole-cloth shade can be made from a piece of fabric no more than 8 by 20 inches. If the lamp shade of your dreams is larger than that, you can piece it in sections, as shown in Figure 11–1, using one or several fabrics.

Silks and silkies work exquisitely well for this use. Because, when the lamp is on, you will be able to see the seams, position them along the wires of the frame and/or toward the back of the shade if it won't be visible from all sides.

You can cover visible seam allowances with strips of dark fabric or bias tape to create a dark line (as in stained glass) rather than a visible seam. Add depth and texture by layering fabrics, always testing for light transmission, of course, and consider using appliqués. One of my all-

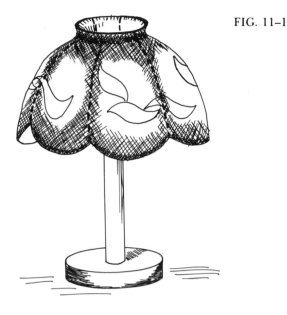

FIG. 11–1

time-favorite lamp shades was a simple one done in shades of blue silk. I lined it with a deep rose red. When the lamp was off, the shade was blue, but when turned on, a rosy glow was created and no blue was perceived at all.

If you're re-covering an existing lamp shade, remove the fabric, paper or whatever and use it for a pattern. If you're working with just a wire frame, it's easy enough to pin your fabric to the frame, mark and cut for a precise fit. And precision isn't demanded, either. A simple gathered tube can look very attractive with almost no fitting needed whatsoever.

Go to an antique store and admire the ornate Victorian loops and swags, fringe and beads, for inspiration. After you've made a simple tailored shade or two, you might want to go for rococo baroque.

PRAIRIE POINT RUGS AND QUILTS

We've already talked about prairie points and how to make them. I would have never considered using these little candy corn constructions underfoot, but recently I saw a rug made of them. It was the essence of simplicity—just rows of points sewed to a sturdy backing.

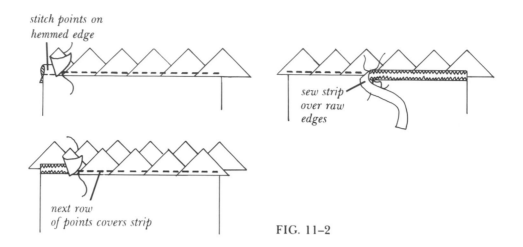

stitch points on hemmed edge

sew strip over raw edges

next row of points covers strip

FIG. 11–2

You'll want to use tough fabrics for this project and squares cut 5 inches or so. Fold either to the center or to the side. In addition to the backing and points, you'll need strips. They can be either cut on the bias or cut straight with edges pressed under. Hem one edge of your backing fabric. Arrange the first row of prairie points along that hemmed edge, with points just covering the hem, as shown in Figure 11–2.

Sew a strip across the raw edges of the points as shown. Straight stitching works fine if you're using pressed strips; if you choose unpressed bias strips, set your machine for zigzag. Arrange the second row so that the points cover the stitched strip, then sew it in place, and so on.

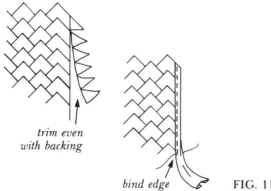

trim even with backing

bind edge

FIG. 11–3

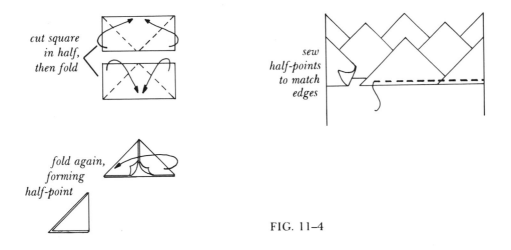

sew
half-points
to match
edges

fold again,
forming
half-point

FIG. 11–4

You can handle the edges one of two ways: Either disregard the irregularity of the edges while you're sewing, then trim to fit the backing and bind those edges (as shown in Fig. 11–3); or make half-points for the edges by cutting your original squares in half, either diagonally or straight. Fold as shown in Figure 11–4.

If you use half-points, it's up to you whether you bind the edges or not. When you've covered the backing, bind the final edge.

Use this same method but lighter weight fabrics to make a beautiful unquilted quilt. Wouldn't multi-colored silk be beautiful, like leaves fallen onto a forest floor?

trash

LET'S TALK TRASH

TRASH FABRICS

We've talked about techniques using strips and bits, and a great many of them also called for trash. Trash can be anything from a bolt of flawed muslin to the embarrassing pieces of a Japanese designer skirt you didn't have the nerve to wear.

Is this a familiar scenario? "It was heavy, it was ugly, it was red-and-white diagonal stripes. It was also 60 inches wide, 100% cotton, imported from France and marked down from $18 to $1 a yard. I hoped the buyer for the store had gone on to another, more appropriate career. I compromised and bought two yards."

Then you know about trash.

One major advantage of working with trash fabrics is that the pieces are usually fairly large — after all, it's easy to throw away a piece of wrinkly chartreuse cotton 3 by 8 inches; it's when you're stuck with a half-yard or so that your frugal Puritan takes over and says, "You can't throw that away." Of course that voice never comes back in with practical advice on what to do with it once you've saved it; am I right?

Our personal preferences, prejudices, if you will, determine our individual definitions of trash fabric. Fiber content and weave are usually major determiners. Don't be hampered by color, because color — indeed the entire fabric — usually disappears between layers of other fabrics.

STRIP-PIECED UNDERLINING

Refer back to Chapters 4 and 5 on strip piecing, and you'll notice right away that strip piecing is done on a backing. Because that backing disappears, it's a perfect way to use trash. Now obviously you're not going to use an acetate jersey or textured wool for this. Strip piecing requires a stable backing, and the eventual use of the piece itself must be considered. Actually, if you were making a jacket or a quilt that would be dry-cleaned, a lightweight wool *would* be quite suitable, but generally for strip piecing you'll want to choose a cotton or poly/cotton blend. Color is immaterial; if your backing is dark or heavily patterned and you have strips of lightweight, light-colored fabrics to apply, all you have to do is double the strip.

In a quilt, it's a good idea to have all your backing squares cut from the same cloth; in a jacket, however, you could use different fabrics to advantage. Choose a cotton flannel for backing the front and back for warmth; use a light broadcloth for the sleeves.

Always pre-wash your backing. Not only will it make the finished item behave more predictably, it makes for much easier sewing if the sizing is removed. Although this is an important consideration in machine sewing, it becomes absolutely vital for hand-sewing techniques such as Afghani piecework.

If you're eager to try strip piecing and find yourself in the unlikely position of having no suitable trash fabric on hand, use the least-worn portions of an old sheet. It's an excellent weave and weight.

INTERFACING

Any fabric can be used as an interfacing; some just do a better job of it than others. There isn't a reason in the world you shouldn't use scrap fabric for interfacing. It doesn't matter whether a fabric is marketed as interfacing or not. Make sure it will behave as you want it to, and pre-shrink it.

Several ways to clean-finish a woven fabric used as interfacing (when the use demands finishing) are: zigzag stitch near the raw edges,

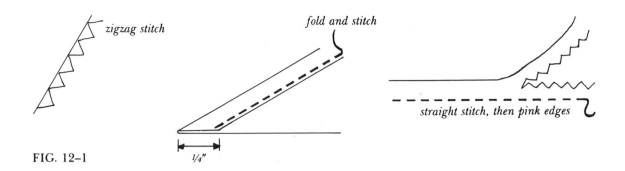

FIG. 12–1

zigzag stitch

fold and stitch

straight stitch, then pink edges

¼"

fold up a scant ¼ inch and straight stitch, or straight stitch and pink. These are all shown in Figure 12–1.

Of course when the interfacing is totally enclosed (as in collars), you'd handle a "trick" interfacing just as you would a proper one.

MORE TRASH

Any tablecloth will lie more smoothly and look better if it is placed over a lining. Because no one will ever see this lining, you can use trash fabric with aplomb. And because it's not attached to the tablecloth, you can replace the lining when you choose. Seam together the light orange, aqua and pea green sleepwear fleece Aunt Eleanor insisted you take. Toss your Christmas print tablecloth over it, and only you will know.

Another household item that requires large amounts of unseen fabric is a dust ruffle for the bed. Instead of buying four yards of muslin for the large hidden area between the mattress and box springs, use your trash. Anything that won't stretch or creep is going to perform just fine in this capacity.

If, after thinking about a piece of trash fabric in this new light, it still seems useless or undesirable, get rid of it fast. You gain the benefits of not seeing it and the space it formerly occupied. There are some hard-core users among us who actually cut or tear trash fabric into tiny bits, who really save ¼-inch trimmings and little shreds, and use them for stuffing.

scrap happy

NOW THAT YOU HAVE SCRAP FEVER. . .

SCRAPS IN THE MAIL

I asked several of my scrap-happy friends to comment on how they deal with scraps. Three of the best letters follow. Claudia Pesek, of Grants Pass, Oregon, designed and markets the Close n Comfy baby carrier, as well as other patterns. She leads off:

"I do save *all* scraps, and they get used for various things like appliqué work (you never know when that odd color of green scrap might come in handy for a tree, flower stem or frog suit!), scrap quilting (of course), of if it's a fairly good size scrap, say ½ yard to a 1 yard piece, I may use it with something else to make a color-coordinated child's item, or placemats. And then there are the flannel scraps. Some fabrics I use so much of, like flannel, that it has a pile of its own. I cut the flannel into 4-inch squares, and they are always ready to sew up into the cuddliest baby blanket that becomes the favorite of the recipient. A majority of the scraps go into a special basket just for my kids to use when they get 'stitch fever.' They never have to ask me if it's okay, and most of the fabrics coordinate, so they can mix and match and get a good eye for color and design elements. They also have a scrap lace box and a scrap paper box. Larger scraps make nice 'seamstress' friend gifts. . .a basket filled with coordinated fabrics, a yard or two of ribbon or lace, and thread. Sometimes I prepare special fabrics like satins, velvets or silks with embroidery thread or something similar to inspire creativity in the receiver. An appliqué pattern I've designed adds a personal touch."

Betty Leuth, from Moline, Illinois, shares recycling and scrap-using tricks:

"To begin with, I place pattern pieces on the fabric to use a lot less than the patterns call for. Their layouts are so wasteful. Sometimes I use the scraps for aprons, doll clothes, sleeveless blouses, make-up bags of padded picture frames. I keep a variety of cardboard squares to cut quilt pieces (1″, 2″, and so on). When I can no longer find what I consider a usable piece, I snip the remaining scraps into tiny pieces to use as stuffing. When I lived in Arkansas, I learned of a challenging and fun way to make a quilt. They called it hit or miss. You use any scrap of material, any shape, and piece them together like a jigsaw puzzle. The fun comes in when you find that you don't have a straight edge to sew the next piece onto. Colors are not taken into consideration unless you have many pieces to choose from. The trick is to come out with straight sides, top and bottom. Some people appliqué a piece on to make it fit. Try not to cut *any* pieces to fit.

"Pieced material can be used for anything you need—clothing, curtains, pillow covers, sachets, padded hanger covers, shoe bags, pot holders, blocks, doll bedding, flannel wash cloths. How about a texture book for baby to chew on. I made a pouch with shoulder straps for Missy's (Betty's daughter) radio. She has mini stereo speakers, and I made a belt with pouches for them. She can go outside wired for sound."

Carol Goddu of Mississauga, Ontario, Canada, sent slides of two beautiful scrap quilts and tells show they came to be:

"At the September 1985 meeting of the Halton Quilters Guild, a member brought in a large garbage bag filled with dressmaker's clippings which had been donated to the guild. Since the fabrics were all silks and silkies they were not considered promising prospects for a quilt. I volunteered to take them and turn them into a quilt. I sorted them by color and added fabrics I already had in the red-purple range.

"The first quilt, 'Compleat Insanity,' (see Color Section) was made as 16 individual blocks strip pieced into three-dimensional pleats, all on the machine. Then each block was cut in three sections and re-assembled, intercutting purple blocks with red blocks. All raw edges were covered with black velvet ribbon.

(The real expense of this project, but the same technique could be used with cotton scraps and bias tape more cheaply.)"

SPECIAL FABRICS

Storing specialty fabrics is often easiest if you let color considerations slide. Keep all your Ultrasuede scraps in a shoebox, all your silk leftovers in an old suitcase.

Most of the fabric we'll talk about in this section can be used with aplomb in all the ways we've covered throughout the book. Let's consider here, then, a few of the unique properties and uses.

People who love Ultrasuede brand fabric really love it, and it is a marvelous material. But did you know that many suedes can also be machine washed and that real leather is as easy to sew as synthetics? Don't overlook the possibilities in using real suede and leather along with your fabric. Ultrasuede, of course, is a natural for appliqué. With no edges to turn under, no raveling to worry about, it's a joy to work with. It's easy to use for belts, straps and trims, yokes and cuffs. Do experiment with a regular needle *and* a wedge-pointed leather needle in sewing leather on your machine.

FIG. 13–1 *Ultrasuede is perfect for appliqués. Kathy Frattaroli of Sterling Heights, Michigan, cut her ballerina bear from Ultrasuede, and satin stitched it to a child's sweatshirt. Scraps of ruffled trim and ribbons complete the bear's ensemble.*

Marta Alto, of Lake Oswego, Oregon, is famous for her speed-sewing techniques and for her work with Ultrasuede. Marta told me that she cuts this miracle fabric into strips ⅛ inch to ¼ inch in width, knots the ends, and uses it for knitting. She mixes the Ultrasuede with yarns for a rich, multi-textured look.

Judi Cull of Sacramento, California, showed me some jackets for men she'd developed in corduroy, using the very quality that drives some of us crazy when working with this fabric. Judi cut and pieced the corduroy together with nap running in different directions. This creates a beautiful, subtle difference in color and sheen. It's especially suitable for menswear, because it's understated and low-key, and men tend to be conservative about wearing custom clothing. No one would raise an eyebrow at these creations: they look classy, not crafty.

Most of us have an old-blue-jeans collection. In addition to the well-known bags and patches denim is perfect for, you can make fine, tough quilts. If you don't mind having a quilt that takes all day to dry, then you'll have no problem at all with a denim quilt. I especially like their who-cares qualities. Throw the quilt down on the grass for baby to crawl on, toss it over a chilly, dirty, sleeping back-yard camper. Who cares? Of course you'll want to keep your blue-jean quilts true to the medium and not get too carried away. Keep it simple, keep it quick.

When I made "Blues for Charlie" (see color section), I knew I wanted to use Ultrasuede and old faded denim, but I didn't know how I'd cope with the thick seams. This was to be graceful, wearable, not a suit of armor. Solving that technical dilemma was rewarding—here's how it came about. I used a muslin backing cut to the approximate shape of the pattern piece, then alternated strips of Ultrasuede and frayed denim (exploiting their non-ravel and already-raveled properties) with strips of woven, broadcloth-weight fabrics. Because a strip of Ultrasuede overlapped a strip of calico, say, no turning under of raw edges was needed at all. Overlapping the calico on its other side would be a strip of frayed denim, and so on.

Jackie Dodson's fringed denim rug is an excellent project that uses up yards and yards of denim quickly. Jackie took a piece of upholstery-weight fabric and finished the edges for a base. She cut bias strips of denim about 2½ inches wide. Using the zipper foot, she set her machine for right needle position. She folded the first strip lengthwise to find the center, opened it up and placed it ⅛ inch from the finished edge of the backing. Then she stitched down the center of the denim strip, adding more strips as needed, to complete the first row. She folded the left side of the strip to the right, pushed the second strip as close as possible to the first, and stitched down the center of the second strip(s). Jackie covered the base fabric this way, then clipped each strip every ½ inch, staggering the clips.

I found myself with a yard or two of wide, coarse-mesh fabric. Well, to be honest, I actually bought this fabric in an unguarded moment. Rather than admit this mesh to the trash category, I cut ¼-inch strips of woven fabrics and threaded them with a safety pin through the mesh at irregular intervals, letting the ends hang toward the front. This resulted in a fine summer curtain, as the woven-in strips create general visual interest and cast shadows.

Look at your specialty fabric scraps with a wise eye. Exploit their unique qualities rather than wrestling them into performing in a way that's foreign to their natural tendencies.

THE FIRST BOLD LINE

Everyone has talent. Everyone is an artist. Well. . .maybe. But we've all seen cartoons of the writer staring at a blank page, the painter at an all-too-white canvas. If acknowledged artists find themselves in this predicament, how much worse could it be for most of us, mere dilettantes, uncomfortable in the very role?

Suppose you dream you're enrolled in a school of art, one of those dreams in which you've missed the first three and three-fourths years of college and show up for your final exams. You have a vaguely guilty feeling that you should know more, a lot more, than you do. You experience the impostor phenomenon: Soon they will discover that you are unqualified, that you do not belong here, that you are a fake. Meanwhile, it's time for your first class.

Doors to two rooms are open, and you look inside, free to choose which class to enter. In the first, people are approaching easels holding huge blank canvases. Neat, unopened tubes of paint are arranged at ev-

NOW THAT YOU HAVE SCRAP FEVER...   **149**

ery easel, dozens of expensive new brushes lie on clean palettes. In the second room, students begin gathering at long tables cluttered with sheets of Masonite, piled with brightly colored bits of paper and fabric. Pots of glue sit conveniently nearby. Music plays in the background, and conversations begin as people reach for materials and begin arranging and considering their collages. You awaken.

Which room would you enter? Why?

At least two factors are heavily involved here, factors which the accomplished artist wouldn't even notice but that can make or break the abiding artist in Everyman—blankness and precious materials. It is easier to combine, to arrange, to manipulate and to rearrange existing materials than to sketch in that first bold line. It is easier to play and to learn with tools and materials that do not intimidate us. Once the ease and expertise are there, the artist in Everyman no longer fears the blank canvas. . .or the silk charmeuse. She joyfully sweeps her brush to form the first bold line.

SO HARD TO SAY GOODBYE

Just as it's difficult for us to bid adieu to our treasured fabrics, it's hard for me to say goodbye to you. There seems to be so much more to say—if I could just wait another week, I'd find the answers to more questions. But time goes on, and this book, anyway, has come to a close.

The purpose of writing *The Fabric Lover's Scrapbook* was to share ways of storing, sorting and using up those scraps. It was also to help me get rid of my scraps. Yet now I'd like to invite more scraps into my life. If you've enjoyed the book and would like to help me build a bridge between us, send me a scrap. I'll put together a charm quilt (we talked about those in Chapter 8) from all the 4-inch squares I receive from you. I've been flirting with the idea of making a charm quilt in red ever since I heard Jinny Beyer's talk at our local quilt guild meeting, and this seems to be the perfect way to go about it. Put as many 4-inch squares (no smaller, please, but I don't mind trimming larger pieces) of different red or red-print fabrics as you like into an envelope and send it to me at P. O. Drawer D, Azle, TX 76020. Sign your squares with permanent marker, if you'd like to. That way, we won't have to say goodbye.

THE SCRAP BAG GALLERY

AROUND THE HOUSE

Folk art for the wall — made in a flash by Linda Stephenson of Bend, Oregon. Linda machine appliquéd simple red hearts and bandana-print bears to a solid-color background, and edged the hoop with lace.

This roadrunner placemat was machine-appliquéd by designer Dorothy Herberg of Rogue River, Oregon. Machine appliqué is one of the fastest and easiest ways to spark up household accessories and make a bold personal statement.

Another good scrap project by Dorothy Herberg, the fabric blackboard. Framed in a contrasting fabric and calico, black cotton makes an eye-catching area to pin up notes, messages and reminders. It's lightly padded with polyester batting.

A basket for use all year 'round. Designer Laura Kluvo of Boca Raton, Florida, combines layers of stuffed fabrics and lace, tops it all off with a strip-pieced heart shape. Ribbons and lace appliqués complete the confection.

Wreaths have become popular for all seasons of the year. Cindy Taylor Oates made this one for Valentine's Day. Negative space between stuffed hearts forms a starburst design.

This kitchen-reminder hoop was machine appliquéd and embroidered by Eileen Westfall of Edmonds, Washington. Hearts, cherries and strawberries circle the pie slice.

Not just your everyday scrap quilt by any stretch of the imagination—yet designer Charlotte Patera of Novato, California, combines pieces of many varied fabrics to produce this "Winter Garden" quilt. It's a masterpiece in hexagonal piecing, standard and reverse appliqué, and hand quilting.

Janet Page-Kessler of New York, New York, created this visual treat which she calls "Jacob's Ladder." Scraps of many different fabrics, including polished cotton, combine to produce subtle variations in color.

CONTAINING THE SITUATION

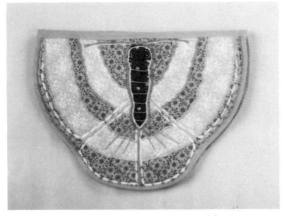

This butterfly cosmetics case was designed by Loretta Daum Byrne. Pieced of floral prints, the case is further embellished with machine embroidery and appliqué. See the case, opened.

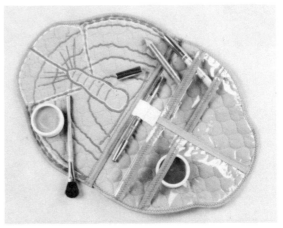

Opened, the butterfly cosmetics case has clear plastic pockets and elastic bands to hold small items.

This handy little tissue case gets added appeal from chicken-scratch embroidery worked on the top. The designer is Mary Polityka Bush of Piedmont, California.

Protect your paperback book and make other people wonder what you're reading. Bethene Larson of Cody, Wyoming, made this simple book cover of corduroy, trimmed with a flower in machine appliqué and embroidery.

Charlyne Stewart of Los Angeles, California, used scraps of Japanese cottons to make her soft box and book cover. She carried the Oriental theme further by working a traditional sashiko-style quilting motif on both.

Carol Krob of Iowa City, Iowa, uses scraps of satin and other fancy fabrics to make little drawstring bags for jewelry or keepsakes. Use waste canvas or iron-on grids to work cross-stitch and beading motifs.

Surely you never lay your eyeglasses down and forget where they are, but if you know someone who does, make them a quilted holder that stays put due to the weights (small peas or beans) in the gathered base. Loretta Daum Byrne designed the holder. Use leftover pieces of pre-quilted fabric or machine quilt two or more layers together.

This lightly padded kitchen owl hangs on the wall to hold wooden utensils or whatever you like. You could use scraps from your curtain fabrics or kitchen chair coverings. Designed by Darline Berry of Sumpter, Oregon.

Know somebody who sews? The little "Armchair Sewing Caddy" by Nancy Foisy of Coos Bay, Oregon, is easy to whip up with scraps of pre-quilted or quilted-by-you fabrics. The center is pleated and stuffed to form a pincushion.

Hang a little sign over the nursery door to warn everyone to quiet down. Theta Happ of Oklahoma City, Oklahoma, worked the design in her charted needle embroidery technique, zigzag stitching over small, double-pointed knitting needles to produce a rich, corduroy-like effect. (See Suggested Reading.)

A quick baby gift made from materials you probably already have around the house — scraps of cotton print, lace and batting. Loretta Byrne embroidered the heart motif with a stylized flower.

Just right for a baby's first doll, this little boy and girl pair were designed by Amy Albert Bloom of Shillington, Pennsylvania. Hair, eyes and heart are machine appliquéd in place, then front and back sewn together, lightly stuffed. Mmmm. . .good to chew on.

Surround your stitchery with a soft ruffle of scrap fabric in a tiny print. This Rock-A-Bye baby pillow is by Denise May-Levenick of Pasadena, California, and has a music box hidden inside to lull baby to sleep.

Dress up a doll with custom clothes. Mary Tudor Smith of Elyria, Ohio, outfits her "September Sweetheart" doll in a felt hat and skirt with appliquéd leaves, adds lace-up shoes and a knitted sweater.

Majel Sullivan of Sherman, Texas, made this hand-puppet mitt for bathtime fun from white terrycloth with gingham appliqués, a fringe of yarn for hair. This one says "Scrub-a-dub-dub, Jump in the tub!" Machine embroidering the child's name on it would be a nice touch.

Dress Teddy or his proud owner in a ready-made sweatshirt or one you've stitched yourself. Cindy Taylor Oates of Scottsdale, Arizona, made this one special with an appliquéd teddy bear cut from a scrap of a quilt. This is a good use for that last corner of an old quilt that's not beautiful enough to frame and treasure but too good just to wrap the punchbowl in.

Kathryn Bergstrom of Santa Rosa, California, often designs on a small scale, making her toys perfect for carrying to church or stuffing in a vacation bag. This little rocking horse is only five inches tall.

Amy Albert Bloom's tiny Japanese sock doll has minimal features and clothing made from scraps of brocade-type fabrics.

A combination of toy and little girl's purse, Barb Forman's Purse*Nalities are simple, flat shapes left open near the heads of the figures to form bags. Barb, of Fort Collins, Colorado, lavishes detail on her work — here the Santa, angel and teddy bear are embroidered, appliquéd and trimmed. Use up scraps, lace, and rickrack.

When this soft game board isn't in use, you can hang it on the wall. Drawstring bag holds playing pieces. It was designed by Pat Cody of Fort Worth, Texas.

Eileen Westfall's machine appliquéd and embroidered hanging strikes a responsive chord among kids and teenagers, and quite a few adults. Chocolate chips, ice cream cones and a cupcake surround the confession. Eileen is from Edmonds, Washington.

WEARABLES

This simple vest is embellished with machine appliquéd pieces of calico, satin and lace. Designer Sandy Dye of Clarion, Pennsylvania, used simple shapes and relied on an assortment of fabrics for interest.

This classic kimono, made from a Folkwear pattern (see Sources of Supply), becomes dramatic with the addition of appliqué. Deanna Charlton of Red Bluff, California, applied the huge blossoms to the dark-colored fabric, then stitched the entire block to the jacket.

Lois Ericson of Tahoe City, California, used strips of fabric in muted shades to embellish this sleeveless jacket. Horizontal strips are stitched and turned, just as you'd sew a sash or strap, held in place only by the vertical, stitched-down strips.

This patternless nomad dress was designed by Catherine Raphael of Rule, Arkansas. A quilt block frames the face; strips trim the sleeves and lower skirt.

Ready for a challenge? After you've become adept at strip piecing, go on to piecing your strips. Deanna Charlton charted the Indian design on the back much like cross-stitch, assembled each strip, then strip pieced the sections.

Not satisfied with simple strip piecing, designer Suzanne McNeill of Fort Worth, Texas, first embellished her fabrics with cross-stitch and Teneriffe embroidery, interspersed fabric strips with lace.

Stuff little curved pocket shapes with cotton or fiberfill, add a handful of potpourri, and tuck them into your shoes to preserve shape and fragrance. Designer, Charlie Davis of Azle, Texas.

Alison Goss of Houston, Texas, who's noted for her fine Seminole piecework, chose the pieced-strip technique for her little girl's vest. Though it's fairly time-consuming and requires concentration, this method is not difficult and produces spectacular results.

Just about as simple as you can get, but adding so much to an ensemble is Gail Brown's silk neck bow. These actually sell in stores for $20 to $30. Give someone a set of three, and you've given an extravagant gift. Gail resides in Aberdeen, Washington.

These bright-eyed Christmas mice by designer Roni Cassista of Panaca, Nevada, are stitched from gray felt. Their tails are braided string, and stuffed circles form their stylized ears. Set on a mantle, hang from the tree, or fill with catnip and give to Fluffy.

If all you want for Christmas is a handful of emeralds, this tiny stocking should be large enough. Mary Polityka Bush of Piedmont, California, cross-stitched selected areas of a gingham stocking, splashed frankly fake jewels across the top.

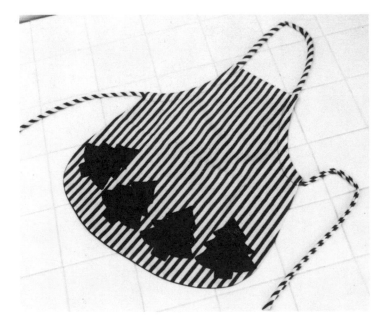

Make a special apron for your favorite cookie baker or apprentice. Chris Pfefferkorn of Plano, Texas, cuts Christmas trees from scraps of green fabric, machine appliqués them to a red and white striped apron.

Joanne Burkhart of Anaheim, California, designed these angels in a variety of sizes. A good use for scraps of holiday print fabrics, angels have flat bases, simple cone-shaped bodies and a variety of trims. Joanne padded the wings lightly; she made curls of hair by wrapping yarn around wooden skewers or metal knitting needles and baking them in a low oven.

Pat Cody's "Angelic Animal" tree ornament features her own pet Scottie dog wearing a halo. Pat, of Fort Worth, Texas, stenciled the design on a padded circle to hang from the tree; it could also be machine appliquéd.

Holly-leaf shapes are stitched wrong sides facing, then stuffed (no turning needed) to form this wreath. Gathered circles make berries, and a bow and white bird complete the project, which is stabilized on the back with a wicker doily. Designer, Pam Nelson of Fridley, Minnesota.

For trick or treat bags or party favors, it's easy to stitch up little drawstring bags. Designer Martie Sandell of Glendale, California, machine appliquéd jack o'lantern faces on these. (See Sources of Supply.)

Masks are a natural for scrap sewing. Here, Loretta Daum Byrne zigzags layers of fabric together to form rows of feathers, then assembles them into an owl mask for Halloween.

This woven basket is made with machine-quilted strips of padded fabric. Designer Constance Hallinan Lagan of North Babylon, New York, makes this version small, to hold a few eggs or candies. The same technique could be used for bigger baskets.

SOURCES OF SUPPLY

Because prices, addresses, and inventory may change from time to time, the best way to contact these suppliers for their current offerings is to write to them and enclose a stamped, self-addressed envelope. Be specific as to your needs and areas of interest. I have had personal experience with all the companies listed here.

SEWING NOTIONS

Clotilde, Inc.
237 S.W. 28th St.
Ft. Lauderdale, FL
　　33315.

One of my all-time favorites. The woman behind the product is evident. Clotilde is constantly finding new tools and methods. Her professional knowledge results in a catalog full of time-savers and performance-improvers, not just gadgets.

The Hands Work
P. O. Box 386
Pecos, NM 87552

High quality, handmade porcelain buttons, jewelry and decorative accessories. A joy. Animals, quilt blocks, cactus—they're all wonderful

Home-Sew
Bethlehem, PA 18018.

This catalog offers general notions like zippers, thread, buttons, dollmaking supplies. Lots of laces and trims are included.

Lacis
2982 Adeline St.
Berkeley, CA 94703.

Specializing in lacemaking tools, this company also deals in general needlecraft books as well as supplies for sewing, knitting, tatting, weaving, and crocheting.

Nancy's Notions, Ltd.
P. O. Box 683
Beaver Dam, WI 53916.

Another big favorite. Nancy is devoted to helping us sew better and faster. You'll find serger supplies, books, interfacings, and all the tools you'll ever need.

Newark Dressmaker
　　Supply, Inc.
P. O. Box 2448
Lehigh Valley, PA
　　18001.

Threads, patterns, dollmaking supplies, trims; a wide variety of sewing supplies at good prices.

Porcupine Pincushion
P. O. Box 1083
McMurray, PA 15317.

You'll find scissors, needles, pressing aids and more in this catalog of sewing notions and craft items.

SewCraft Box 6146 South Bend, IN 46660	A source of hard-to-find notions, plus a newsletter to keep you up-to-date on new developments.
Speed Stitch, Inc. PO Box 3472 Port Charlotte, FL 33952	Books, notions, whatever you might need for sewing.
Western Trading Post P. O. Box 9070 Denver, CO 80209-0070.	Specializing in Indian craft supplies, this catalog also offers a wide selection of beads, adhesives, tools and books.
The World in Stitches 82 South St. Milford, NH 03055.	The ultimate in embroidery supplies. Simply everything, from the common to the esoteric. Evenweave fabrics, silk gauze, precious metallic threads.

See also Aardvark and Treadleart listings, under "Periodicals."

TOOLS AND GADGETS

Birdhouse Enterprises 110 Jennings Ave. Patchogue, NY 11772.	Russian punchneedles, embroidery supplies and patterns.
Braid-Aids 466 Washington St. Pembroke, MA 02359.	Rug braiding tools and accessories.
Craftsman Studio P. O. Box 351 Kennebunkport, ME 04046.	Rug hooks, frames, patterns for hooked rugs, fabrics and Cushing dyes.
For Kids Only P. O. Box 1290 Coos Bay, OR 97420.	Marketers of the Quickie Curlie doll hair maker, a hairpin-lace loom device.
Kaye's Artistic Stitchery 4949 Rau Rd. W. Branch, MI 48661.	Plastic quilting tools called Starmakers make complex quilting designs quick and easy. Also books.
Kleids Enterprises, Inc. P.O. Box 365 Short Hills, NJ 07078	Marketers of weaving sticks and instructions.
Libby's Creations 866 W. Isabella Ave. Mesa, AZ 85202.	Libby's the inventor of the Spool-It, a handy little gadget that fits over your sewing machine's spool pins and enables you to use non-conventional spools of thread.

Love & Money Crafts P. O. Box 987 Ann Arbor, MI 48106.	Plastic looms, called LapWeaving sets, are fine for yarn work, and can be used in limited ways with fabric strips.
Shaggy Spinners, Inc. 1800 N.W. 137th Ave. Portland, Or 97229.	Marketers of the Shaggy Spinner, a hairpin-lace loom with sturdy base, easy to use.
Theta's School of Sewing 2508 N.W. 39th St. Oklahoma City, OK 73112.	Sells supplies needed for charted needle embroidery (machine satin stitching over knitting needles). Curved and straight needles, plus charts and instructions.

PATTERNS AND INSTRUCTIONS

Artful Illusions P. O. Box 278 Ector, TX 75439-0278.	Delightful designs, clear directions for fabric plants and wearables.
Aunt Philly's Tooth- brush Rugs P. O. Box 36335 Denver, CO 80236.	Directions for making several shapes of rugs from fabric strips.
Creative Makings by Martie P. O. Box 4445 Glendale, CA 91202.	Good, easy patterns for holiday items, things for kids, and more.
Design Originals 401 N. Bailey B Ft. Worth, TX 76107.	Instructions for rag baskets, needlepoint rag rugs, wreaths and home furnishings.
Folkwear Patterns P. O. Box 3798 San Rafael, CA 94912.	Absolutely the best in vintage and ethnic clothing patterns, all multi-sized and printed on heavy paper. Includes historical details.
Libby's Creations (see listing under Tools and Gadgets).	Floral and animal appliqué patterns, also appliqué booklets.
Little Lotus 302 Spring St. Cambridge, MI 53523.	Loretta Daum Byrne's inimitable doll patterns, including miniatures.
Yvonne Porcella 3619 Shoemake Ave. Modesto, CA 95351	Vest and jacket patterns with the Porcella touch.

Sew-Art International
P. O. Box 550
Bountiful, UT 84010.

Scads of patterns, directions and supplies for machine embroidery.

Marinda Stewart
P.O. Box 402
Walnut Creek, CA
    94596.

Patterns for sewn and knitted garments, including the original T-dress.

Taylor-Made Designs
P. O. Box 31024
Phoenix, AZ 85046.

Patterns for patchwork sweatshirts and other wearables, quilts.

Tomorrow's Heirlooms
1301 W. Highway 407
Suite 202
Lewisville, TX 75067.

Detailed instructions for meadow points and patterns for skirt, collar and collections of ornaments made with this technique.

FABRICS

Fabrics by Lineweaver
3300 Battleground Ave.
Suite 301
Greensboro, NC 27410.

Mainstream fashion fabrics, nice catalog.

Gutcheon Patchworks,
    Inc.
611 Broadway,
Room 201
New York, NY 10012.

Polished cottons, cotton prints, also books, notions, supplies.

Kieffer's Lingerie Fabrics and Supplies
1625 Hennepin Ave.
Minneapolis, MN
    55403.

Lingerie fabrics, laces, swimsuit fabrics. Good prices.

Mini-Magic
3675 Reed Rd.
Columbus, OH 43220.

Specializing in dollmaking and miniature supplies, they also have a wide range of fabrics, laces, threads and trims.

Pennywise Fabrics
Rt. 1, Box 305
Harrisburg, MO 65256.

Penny's fabric prices are almost too good to be true. Natural fibers, no-frills presentation.

Thai Silks!
252 State St.
Los Altos, CA 94022.

Can you afford to sew with silk? I couldn't, if it weren't for this company. The most reasonably priced, quality silk fabrics (some wools, cotton batiks) around.

LEATHER AND ULTRASUEDE

Clearbrook Woolen Shop
P. O. Box 8
Clearbrook, VA 22624.

Ultrasuede scraps at good prices, and as the name implies, fine woolens.

Clotilde, Inc. (see listing under Sewing Notions).

Also sells Ultrasuede scraps, collars, etc.

Nor-Mar Fabrics & Gifts
1327 Main St.
Napa, CA 94559.

Ultrasuede scraps and larger pieces.

Tandy Leather Co.
P. O. Box 2934
Ft. Worth, TX 76113.

Garment-weight leather, washable suedes, snakeskin, shearling.

MISCELLANEOUS

Craftsman Studio (see listing under Tools and Gadgets).

A source for Cushing dyes.

Ivy Crafts Imports
5410 Annapolis Rd.
Bladensburg, MD 20710.

Silk-painting supplies, fabrics, instructions.

Joyce's Creations
5601 Edgewater Circle
Rowlett, TX 75088.

Beautiful porcelain replicas of antique dolls (see Fig. 10–9). Joyce and Ken Ensey are national prize-winners, have a large selection of dolls.

Savoir-Faire
P. O. Box 2021
Sausalito, CA 94966.

Complete line of silk-painting supplies.

PERIODICALS

Aardvark Territorial Enterprize
P. O. Box 2449
Livermore, CA 94550.

More than a newsletter, more than a catalog, more like a creative network for stitchers.

American Craft
American Craft Council
401 Park Ave. South
New York, NY 10016.

Glossy, expensive review of needlecraft and pottery, wood, metal, etc.

Cerulean Blue
P. O. Box 21168
Seattle, WA
     98111-3168.

It's really a catalog, but it's also a showcase for what's being done in color in the fiber arts, a how-to guide for the dyer/painter of fabric, a sourcebook for tools, fabrics, dyes.

Fiberarts
50 College St.
Asheville, NC 28801.

An overview of fiber arts, just as the title says. A fine magazine.

Needlecraft for Today
4949 Byers
Ft. Worth, TX 76107

Excellent how-to magazine covering knit, crochet, sewing, surface design, embroidery, needlepoint. (I say it's excellent, but then I'm one of the editors.)

Quilter's Newsletter
6700 W. 44th Ave.
Wheatridge, CO 80033.

One of the few publications I'll stop whatever I'm doing to browse through, if not read cover to cover. Some how-to, lots of overview.

Rug Hooker News &
     Views
P. O. Box 351
Kennebunkport, ME
     04046.

If you've never hooked a rug in your life, this magazine will make you want to start one.

Sew News
P. O. Box 1790
News Plaza
Peoria, IL 61656.

Lots of fashion forecasts, information mainly for dressmaker-type stitchers.

Surface Design
311 E. Washington St.
Fayetteville, TN 37334.

The best in dying, stamping, painting on fabrics and other surfaces. Good source of inspiration.

Threads
Box 355
Newtown, CT 06470.

Classy magazine dealing with every aspect of needlecraft, profiles artists working in our field.

Treadleart
25834-I Narbonne Ave.
Lomita, CA 90717.

Projects and updates in the machine embroidery field.

SUGGESTED READING

APPLIQUE

Forman, Barb, *Pizzazz for Pennies*, Chilton Book Co., 1986.
Patera, Charlotte, *Cutwork Applique*, New Century Publishers, Inc., 1983.
_____, *Mola Making*, New Century Publishers, Inc., 1984.
Perna, Sharon, *Machine Applique*, Sterling Publishing Co., Inc. 1986.

CHAIR SEAT WEAVING

Sober, Marion Burr, *Chair Seat Weaving for Antique Chairs*, Finestkind Books, 1964; reissued 1986. Available from Connecticut Cane & Reed Co., Box 762, Manchester, CT 06040.

CLOTHING

Avery, Virginia, *Quilts to Wear*, Scribner's, 1983.
Dale, Julie Schafler, *Art to Wear*, Abbeville Press, 1986.
Ericson, Lois, *Belts*, Eric's Press, 1984.
_____, *Belts. . .Waisted Sculpture*, Eric's Press, 1984.
Locke, Sue, *Learn to Make Children's Clothes*, The Main Street Press, 1987.
Martin, Karen Ericsson, *Angel Threads (Creating Lovable Clothes for Little Ones)*, Lark Books, 1986.
Porcella, Yvonne, *Pieced Clothing*, Porcella Studios, 1980.
_____, *Pieced Clothing Variations*, Porcella Studios, 1981.
Thompson, Sue, *Decorative Dressmaking*, Rodale Press, 1985.

DESIGN

Ericson, Lois, *Fabrics. . .Reconstructed*, Eric's Press, 1985.
Ericson, Lois and Diane, *Ethnic Costume*, Van Nostrand Reinhold, 1979.

Ericson, Lois and Frode, Diane Ericson, *Design & Sew It Yourself*, Eric's Press, 1983.

Mattera, Joanne (editor), *The Quiltmaker's Art*, Lark Books, 1981.

McMorris, Penny, and Kile, Michael, *The Art Quilt*, The Quilt Digest Press, 1986.

Porcella, Yvonne, *A Colorful Book*, Porcella Studios, 1986.

Robinson, Charlotte (editor), *The Artist & The Quilt*, Alfred A. Knopf, 1983.

EMBROIDERY

Bird, Gail, *Russian Punchneedle Embroidery*, Dover Publications, Inc., 1981.

Bond, Dorothy, *Crazy Quilt Stitches*, Self-published (Dorothy Bond, 34706 Row River Road, Cottage Grove, Oregon 97424), 1981.

Brown, Marinda, *Ideas & Inspirations, (A Punchneedle Techniques Primer)*, Self-published (Marinda Brown, 2512 Tulare Ave., El Cerrito, CA 94530), 1983.

Carroll, Mary, *Making Needlecraft Landscapes*, St. Martin's Press, 1986.

Fanning, Robbie and Tony, *The Complete Book of Machine Embroidery*, Chilton Book Co., 1986.

Stiles, Phyllis, *Not Just Another Embroidery Book*, Lark Books, 1986.

GENERAL

Fulton, Alice and Hatch, Pauline, *It's Here. . .Somewhere*, Writer's Digest Books, 1986.

Laury, Jean Ray, *The Creative Woman's Getting-It-All-Together-at-Home Handbook*, Van Nostrand Reinhold, 1977.

Snyder, Grace, *No Time on My Hands*, University of Nebraska Press, 1963, 1986. (Foreword and epilogue by Nellie Snyder Yost.)

von Oech, Roger, *A Whack on the Side of the Head*, Warner Books, 1983.

QUILTING

Beyer, Jenny, *The Scrap Look*, EPM Publications, Inc., 1985.

Binney, Edwin 3rd, and Binney-Winslow, Gail, *Homage to Amanda*, RK Press, 1984.

Carmack, Doris, *Easy Biscuit Quilting*, Designs by Doris, 1985.

Conroy, Mary, *The Complete Book of Crazy Patchwork*, Sterling Publishing Co., Inc., 1985.

Hargrave, Harriet, *Heirloom Machine Quilting*, Yours Truly, 1987.

Haywood, Dixie, *Crazy Quilt Patchwork*, Dover Publications, Inc., 1981.

———, *Crazy Quilting with a Difference*, Scissortail Publications, 1981.

Hopkins, Mary Ellen, *The It's OK if You Sit on my Quilt Book*, Yours Truly, Inc. 1982.

Hughes, Trudie, *Template-Free Quiltmaking*, That Patchwork Place, Inc., 1986.
_____, *More Template-Free Quiltmaking*, That Patchwork Place, Inc., 1987.
Leman, Bonnie, and Townsend, Louise O., *How to Make a Quilt* (25 Easy Lessons for Beginners), Moon Over the Mountain Publishing Co., 1971; second revised edition 1986.
Logan, Diann, *Designs in Patchwork*, Oxmoor House, 1987.
Martin, Judy, *Scrap Quilts*, Moon Over the Mountain Publishing Company, 1985.
Martin, Nancy J., *Pieces of the Past*, That Patchwork Place, Inc., 1986.
Nephew, Sara, *Quilts from a Different Angle*, That Patchwork Place, Inc. 1986.
Parker, Kay, *Contemporary Quilts* (original patterns based on the drawings of M. C. Escher), The Crossing Press, 1981.
Pasquini, Katie, *Mandala*, Sudz Publishing, 1983.
Puckett, Marjorie, *Shadow Quilting*, Charles Scribner's Sons, 1986.
Schlotzhauer, Joyce M., *The Curved Two-Patch System*, EPM Publications, Inc., 1982.
Stewart, Charlyne Jaffe, *Snowflakes in the Sun* (a how-to guide to Hawaiian quiltmaking), Wallace-Homestead Book Co., 1986.
Swim, Laurie, *The Joy of Quilting*, Harlow Publishing, Inc., 1984.
Syme, Lynette-Merlin, *Learn Patchwork*, The Main Street Press, 1987.
Wein, Carol Anne, *The Great American Log Cabin Quilt Book*, E. P. Dutton, Inc., 1984.
Wood, Kaye, *Quilt Like A Pro*, Extra Special Products, Inc., 1983.
Wright, Sandra Lee (editor), *Quilts From Happy Hands*, Happy Hands Publishing Co., 1981.

RUGS

Cary, Sally Clarke, *How to Make Braided Rugs*, McGraw-Hill, 1977.
Ketchum William C., Jr., *Hooked Rugs*, Harcourt, Brace Jovanovich, Inc., 1976.
Moshimer, Joan, *The Complete Rug Hooker (A Guide to the Craft)*, Leith Publications, 1975.
_____, *Treasury of Hooked Rug Designs*, W. Cushing & Co., Inc., 1976.
Seigfreid, Mary E., *Primitive Rug Hooking: Making Heirlooms for Today's Home*, Hobby House Press, Inc., 1987. (Directions for seven small "non-rug" hooked items).

SCRAPCRAFT

Allison, Linda and Stella, *Rags: Making a Little Something Out of Almost Nothing*, Clarkson N. Potter, Inc., 1979.
Foose, Sandra Lounsbury, *Scrap Saver's Stitchery Book*, Countryside Press, 1977.
_____, *More Scrap Saver's Stitchery*, Farm Journal, Inc., 1981.
_____, *Scrap Saver's Gift Stitchery*, Sedgewood Press, 1984.

SEMINOLE PIECEWORK

Seminole Research/Design Project, *Seminole Patchwork Principles and Designs*, Self-published, 1980.

SEWING

Betzina, Sandra, *Power Sewing*, Self-published, 1985.

Brown, Gail, *Sensational Silk*, Palmer/Pletsch, 1982.

Clotilde and Lawrence, Judy, *Sew Smart*, IBC Publishing Co., 1982.

Dodson, Jackie, *Know Your Bernina*, Chilton Book Co., 1987.

Eaton, Jan, *The Encyclopedia of Sewing Techniques*, Barron's, 1987.

Hall, Carolyn, *The Sewing Machine Craft Book*, Van Nostrand Reinhold, 1980.

Mansour, Diana (editor), *Decorative Home Sewing (French Chic)*, Ballantine Books, 1987.

Palmer, Pati and Pletsch, Susan, *Mother Pletsch's Painless Sewing*, Palmer/Pletsch Associates, 1975.

Zieman, Nancy, *The Busy Woman's Sewing Book*, Nancy's Notions, Ltd., 1984.

INDEX

Entries in **bold** list fabric descriptions and project categories. For instance, if you have an abundance of velveteen scraps, look under **Velvet, velveteen**, and you'll find a listing of projects, ideas, photographs and illustrations suitable for making with velveteen. If you need to make a gift for a man, look under **Men and boys** for suitable projects. *Italic* page numbers indicate information in illustrations.